Home for the Holidays

Lynda Milligan & Nancy Smith

Dedication

We would like to dedicate this book to Christine Scott. Chris has worked for us for over ten years in our receiving area which includes kit making, packing and organizing trade shows, and scheduling trunk shows. An excellent quilting teacher, she has introduced the arts of piecing, applique, and quilting to hundreds of new quilters. Her great color sense is apparent in all her work.

One of Chris' greatest assets is her attention to detail. She spends many hours proofing our books and is one of the reasons they are virtually error-free.

In her free time, Chris enjoys knitting and quilting for her two daughters, sons-in-law, and four precious grandchildren. Thanks, Chris, for your hard work and dedication.

Credits

Sharon Holmes – Editor, Technical Illustrator
Lexie Foster – Cover, Illustration, Quilt Design, Photo Stylist
Susan Johnson – Quilt Design, Photo Stylist
Christine Scott – Editorial Assistant
Sandi Fruehling – Copy Reader
Brad Bartholomew – Photographer

Thanks

Sewing & Machine Quilting – Ann Petersen, Jane Dumler,
Katie Wells, Courtenay Hughes, Susan Auskaps, Sue Williams
Long-arm Machine Quilting – Sandi Fruehling, Susan F. Geddes, Carolyn Schmitt

POSSIBILITIES®

…Fabric designers for AvLyn Inc., publishers of DreamSpinners®
patterns & I'll Teach Myself® & Possibilities® books…
Home of Great American Quilt Factory, Inc.

Snow Buddy

Photo on page 3   Finished size approximately 30 x 63"

Materials Choose fabric with 42" usable width.

Light brown	½ yd	snowman background, upper
Creams	⅛ yd each of 3	snowman background, lower
Whites	¼ yd each of 4	snowman body
Blues	⅛ yd each of 3	small trees background
Tans	¼ yd each of 5	large trees background
Greens	½ yd each of 5	large & small trees, prairie points, center panel border
Green	⅓ yd	checkerboard
Brown	¼ yd	houses, small tree trunks
Dark red	⅓ yd	house roofs, chimneys, top & bottom borders
Dark red	¼ yd	house block sashing, narrow border
Cream	⅜ yd	sky of house blocks, checkerboard
Yellow	⅛ yd	doors, windows of house blocks
Appliques	⅙ yd	vest
	⅛ yd each of 7-9	hat, nose, scarf, arms, vest decoration
Backing	2¼ yd	includes facing
Batting	36 x 69"	
Buttons	2 medium for eyes, 5 tiny for mouth, 4 medium for body	

Cutting When 'strips' appears, cut selvage to selvage.

Light brown	snowman background, upper - 1 piece 13¼ x 20½"
Creams	snowman background, lower - 2 pieces 2½ x 21¼", 1 piece 2¾ x 21¼"
Whites	snowman body - 13 strips 1½" wide
Blues	small trees background - paper piecing, see Directions, Step 2
Tans	large trees background - 12 pieces each: Row 1, top - 2½ x 5½"; Row 2 - 2½ x 4½"; Row 3 - 2½ x 3½"; Row 4 - 2½ x 2½"; Row 5, bottom - 2½ x 4¾"
Greens	large trees - 6 pieces each: Row 1, top - 2½ x 4½"; Row 2 - 2½ x 6½"; Row 3 - 2½ x 8½"; Row 4 - 2½ x 10½"; Row 5, bottom - 2½ x 2"
	small trees - paper piecing, see Directions, Step 2
	prairie points - 14 squares 5½"
	center panel border - 2 pieces 1⅜ x 23", 2 pieces 1⅜ x 26¾"
Green	checkerboard - 3 strips 2⅜" wide
Brown	house - 8 pieces 2 x 5½", 4 pieces 1¾ x 3", 2 pieces 1¾ x 2"
	small trees - paper piecing - see Directions, Step 2
Dark red	house roofs - 2 pieces 3½ x 10½", chimneys - 2 pieces 1½ x 2"
	top & bottom borders - 2 pieces 2½ x 30½"
Dark red	house block sashing - 1 piece 1¼ x 9½", 2 pieces 1⅜ x 9½", 2 pieces 1⅜ x 23"
	narrow border - 1⅛ x 23"
Cream	sky of house blocks - 4 squares 3½", 2 pieces 1½ x 6", 2 pieces 1½ x 3½"
	checkerboard - 3 strips 2⅜" wide
Yellow	doors, windows - 2 pieces 2 x 4¼", 2 squares 3"
Appliques	patterns on pages 59-60
Facing	3 strips 2" wide on lengthwise grain - set aside remaining fabric for backing

Continued on page 28

Family Traditions

How delightful it is to provide our children with Christmas traditions.

Our Favorite Books to Read Aloud:
The Night Before Christmas by Clement Moore, and A Christmas Memory by Truman Capote.

The Giving Tree:
Book stores often have giving trees in the children's section where children can select special books to give to kids in need.

Christmas Eve Drive:
Take a leisurely drive to enjoy all the festive lights around town.

Snow Buddy, page 2. Snow Buddy Tree Skirt, page 29. Snow Buddy Pillows, page 30.

Holly Baskets

Photo on page 5   Finished size approximately 60x74"   10" Block

Yardage Choose fabric with 42" usable width.

Brown	2⅜ yd	baskets, Border 2, Border 3
Tan	1¾ yd	setting squares, triangles
Cream	2½ yd	block background, Border 1, Border 2
Applique	⅛ yd red, ⅜ yd green	berries, leaves
Binding	⅔ yd	
Backing	4 yd	
Batting	66x80"	

Cutting When "strips" appears, cut crossgrain strips (selvage to selvage).
*Cut these squares in **half** diagonally. **Cut these squares in **quarters** diagonally.

Brown	*54 squares 2⅞", *6 squares 6⅞" - baskets
	*55 squares 2⅞" - Border 2
	7 strips 4½" wide - Border 3
Tan	6 squares 10½", **3 squares 15⅜", *2 squares 8"
Cream	*42 squares 2⅞", *6 squares 6⅞", 24 pieces 2½ x 6½", *6 squares 4⅞"
	6 strips 3¼" wide for Border 1 - *55 squares 2⅞", 4 squares 2½" for Border 2
Applique	36 leaves & 36 berries - patterns on page 58
Binding	7-8 strips 2½" wide

Directions Use ¼" seam allowance unless otherwise noted.

1. BLOCKS: Make 12 blocks as shown. Press. Applique holly to each block.

2. ASSEMBLE: Arrange blocks, setting squares and setting triangles as shown. Stitch into diagonal rows. Stitch rows together. Press.

3. BORDER 1: Make 2 side borders by piecing strips to same length as quilt. Stitch to quilt. Press. Repeat at top and bottom.

4. BORDER 2: Make 110 half-square triangle units. Press. Stitch into borders as shown. Press. Stitch side borders to quilt. Press. Repeat with top and bottom borders.

5. BORDER 3: Repeat Step 3.

6. FINISH: Piece backing horizontally to same size as batting. Layer, baste, and quilt. Trim batting and backing even with quilt top. Bind quilt using ⅜" seam allowance.

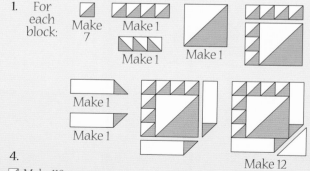

1. For each block:
Make 7   Make 1   Make 1
Make 1
Make 1
Make 1
Make 1
Make 12

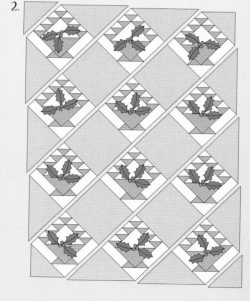
2.

4.
Make 110

Make 2 for sides using 31 half-square triangle units (asymmetrical - 15 on 1 side of center, 16 on other)

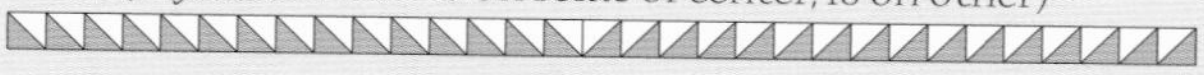

Make 2 for top and bottom using 24 half-square triangle units & 2 cream squares (2½")

Holly Baskets, page 4.

Starry Starry Night

Photo on page 7   Finished size approximately 57x70"   10" Block

Yardage Choose fabric with 42" usable width.

Blues	⅓ yd each of 18 or more
Yellows	¼ yd each of 18 or more
Borders 1 & 2	⅞ yd medium blue
Border 2	¾ yd dark blue
Binding	⅝ yd
Backing	3¾ yd
Batting	63x76"

Cutting When "strips" appears, cut crossgrain strips (selvage to selvage). *Cut these squares in **half** diagonally.

Blues	31 pieces 3½x10½" for sashing, 12 squares 3½" for sashing - remaining fabric is for paper piecing large stars
Yellows	96 squares 2" for small stars - remaining fabric is for paper piecing large stars
Border 1	6 strips 1½" wide - medium blue
Border 2	*36 squares 3⅞" - medium blue
	6 squares 3½", 2 pieces 3½x4½", *36 squares 3⅞" - dark blue
Binding	7 strips 2¼" wide

Directions Use ¼" seam allowance unless otherwise noted.

1. BLOCKS: Paper piece 20 blocks as shown using patterns on pages 55, 56, and 57.

2. SASHING: Make sashing units by stitching yellow squares to corners of blue rectangles. If desired, trim seam allowance to ¼". Press.

3. ASSEMBLE: Arrange blocks and sashing as shown. Stitch into horizontal rows. Stitch rows together. Press. See diagram on page 32.

4. BORDER 1: Make 2 side borders by piecing strips to same length as quilt. Stitch to quilt. Press. Repeat at top and bottom.

5. BORDER 2: Make 72 half-square triangle units. Press. Stitch into 2 side and 2 top/bottom borders as shown using 3½" squares at center and ends of top and bottom borders and 3½x4½" rectangles at center of side borders. Adjust borders to fit at center square or rectangle. Press. Stitch side borders to quilt. Press. Repeat at top and bottom.

6. FINISH: Piece backing horizontally to same size as batting. Layer, baste, and quilt. Trim batting and backing even with quilt top. Bind quilt using ¼" seam allowance.

1.

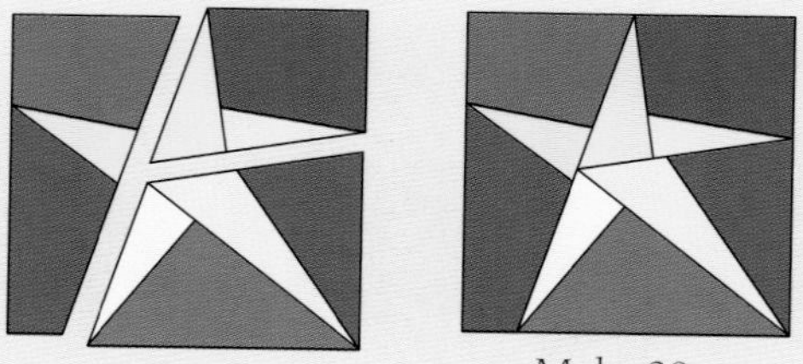

Make 20

2.

Make 14   Make 17

Wine Bottle Wraps

Dress up a gift of wine or champagne with our quick and easy bottle wraps.

★ Cut 2 pieces 4-6x11" of fabric and fuse, wrong sides together. Trim with decorative-edge scissors.

★ Decorate wrap with buttons, charms, sequins, or fused appliques.

★ Tie a few strands of raffia or ribbon around the top and bottom of the wrap to hold it in place.

★ Hang a star or a miniature ornament along with a gift tag around the neck of the bottle.

Gift tag patterns on page 46.

Photo on page 7.

6

Continued on page 32

Starry Starry Night, page 6. Holiday Crackers, page 24. Wine Bottle Wraps, page 6. Gift Tags, page 46.

Strippy Trees

Photo on page 9   Finished size approximately 50x66"   8x10" & 4x5" Blocks

Yardage Choose fabric with 42" usable width.

Trees	⅔ yd each of 10 - medium & dark green
	⅛ yd each dark pink, dark purple
Backgrounds	½ yd each of 11 - 4 lt blue, 2 lt green, 2 lt gold, 2 med purples, 1 med pink
Trunks	¼ yd brown
Border 1	⅜ yd
Border 2	⅝ yd
Binding	⅝ yd
Backing	3⅜ yd
Batting	56x72"

Cutting When 'strips' appears, cut selvage to selvage.

Trees	greens - 1½"–2½" strips in ¼" increments - start with 1 strip of each width of each fabric - remaining fabric is for plain sides of big trees & both sides of small trees
	pink & purple - start with 1 strip 1" wide & 1 strip 1½" wide of each
Backgrounds	blues - use for paper piecing small trees
	other colors - **for 2 large blocks** cut 2 pieces 5½x11"; place **right sides together**; cut in half diagonally (use for paper piecing); cut 4 pieces 2½x4" for trunk units
Trunks	24 pieces 1½x2½" for large tree trunk units (trunk units of large trees are not paper pieced) - remaining fabric is for paper piecing small trees
Border 1	6 strips 1½" wide
Border 2	6 strips 2½" wide
Binding	7 strips 2½" wide

Directions Use ¼" seam allowance unless otherwise noted.

1. BLOCKS: Make 36 copies of paper piecing pattern on page 59. Make 1 copy each of paper piecing patterns on pages 45 and 46, tape halves together, then make 24 copies of full-sized pattern.

    BLOCK A - Paper piece 36 blocks using light blues for background.

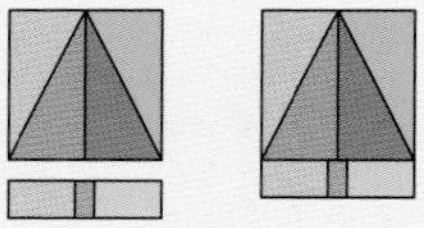

    BLOCK B - Trace diagonal tree lines to wrong side of 10 patterns. String piece full center section on traced side of pattern. Slant strips as desired. Paper piece background triangles to unit using light greens, golds, purples, and pinks. Piece 10 trunk units. Stitch trunk units to top units. Press.

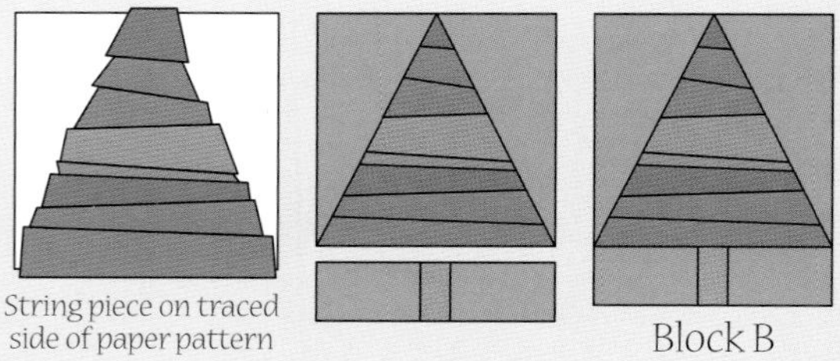

    BLOCK C - Trace diagonal and center vertical tree lines to wrong side of 14 patterns. String piece tree units on traced side, covering half of center section—sometimes left side, sometimes right. Slant strips as desired. Paper piece plain side of tree with greens, then backgrounds using light greens, golds, pinks, and purples. Piece 14 trunk units. Stitch trunk units to top units. Press.

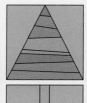

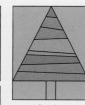

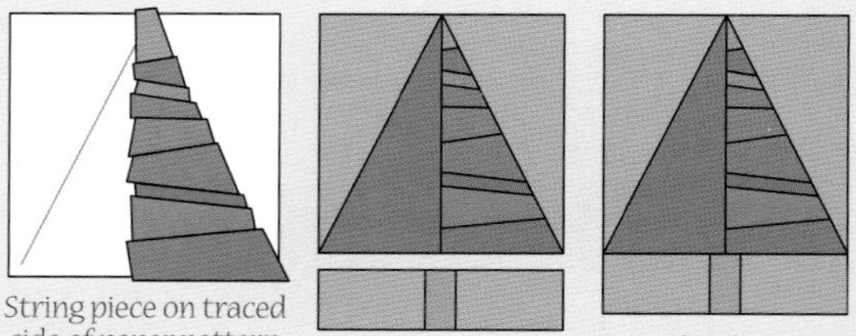

Block A

String piece on traced side of paper pattern

Block B

String piece on traced side of paper pattern

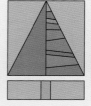

Block C

Continued on page 32

Gift Bags

Give gifts with pizazz and individuality. Readymade gift bags are so easy to personalize!

★ For gifts from the kitchen, cut a circle or heart from the front of a colored lunch bag, then glue a piece of clear plastic inside bag behind hole. Glue recipe to back of bag, fold down top, and seal with a sticker or bow.

★ For that special someone, use ribbon or raffia to tie bag handles together. Let colored tissue or shredded foil peek out from top of bag. Hang gift tag and charms or mini ornaments from ribbon streamers.

Photos on pages 9 and 13.

Strippy Trees, page 8. Gift Bags, page 8.

Kaleidoscope

A Cozy Present

A great idea for a quick and cozy present:

★ Purchase a fleece blanket or throw.

★ Select an applique pattern from the back of this book. Carefully fuse to one corner of the fleece throw using a pressing cloth and very little pressure on the iron.

★ Secure the edges of the applique with machine stitching. Add a wide binding in a coordinating fabric.

★ Tie a ribbon around the tightly-rolled blanket.

Photo on page 11.

Photo on page 11   Finished size approximately 50 x 66"   12" Block Point to Point

Yardage
Choose fabric with 42" usable width.

Greens	½ yd each of 10 fabrics
	OR 1 roll of 20 strips 6½" wide - 2 strips each of 10 greens
Red	¼ yd - blocks
Black	⅞ yd - setting triangles
Border 1	⅓ yd
Border 2	⅝ yd
Border 3	⅞ yd
Binding	⅝ yd
Backing	3⅜ yd
Batting	56 x 72"

Cutting
When 'strips' appears, cut selvage to selvage.

Greens - if using ½-yd cuts	from each fabric - 1 strip 1¼", 1 strip 1½", 1 strip 1¾", 1 strip 2", 1 strip 2½", 1 strip 2¾"
Greens - if using roll of 20 strips	from each of 10 strips - 1 strip 1¼", 1 strip 2", 1 strip 2¾"
	from remaining 10 strips - 1 strip 1½", 1 strip 1¾", 1 strip 2½"
Red	4 strips 1" wide - blocks
Black	24 full triangles, 6 half triangles, 6 half triangles reversed - patterns on page 33
Border 1	5 strips 1½" wide
Border 2	6 strips 2½" wide
Border 3	6 strips 4½" wide
Binding	7 strips 2½" wide

Directions
Use ¼" seam allowance unless otherwise noted.

1. BLOCKS:

    Make 10 strip sets using 1 strip of each width in each set, and adding 1 red strip to 4 of the strip sets in a different position each time. Press.

    Cut out 5 full triangles along one side of strip set. For variety, along other side of strip set, cut out 5 more in different positions. Pattern on page 33.

    Make 13 whole blocks and 4 half blocks as shown on page 33. Press. Trim half blocks leaving ¼" seam allowance.

1.

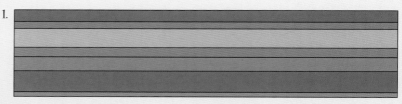

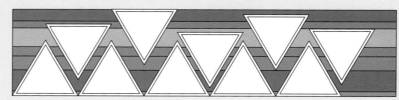

     Continued on page 33

Kaleidoscope, page 10. Stockings, pages 43-44. Fleece Throw, page 10.

Arctic Crystals

Photo on page 13   Finished size approximately 52 x 64"   6" Block

Yardage Choose fabric with 42" usable width.

Blocks, Border 2	¼ yd each of 20 fabrics - 10 greens, 10 blue/purple
	OR 1 roll of 20 strips 6½" wide - 10 green, 10 blue/purple
Border 1	½ yd
Border 3	⅞ yd
Binding	⅝ yd
Backing	3½ yd
Batting	58 x 70"

Cutting When 'strips' appears, cut selvage to selvage.

Blocks, Border 2	from each fabric - 1 strip 2½" wide, 1 strip 2⅞" wide
Border 1	5 strips 2½" wide
Border 3	6 strips 4½" wide
Binding	7 strips 2½" wide

Directions Use ¼" seam allowance unless otherwise noted.

1. BLOCKS: Cut 2½" strips into 2½" squares.

    Cut 2⅞" strips into 2⅞" squares. Cut 2⅞" squares in **half** diagonally. Make 236 half-square triangle units using green on one side and blue on the other. Press. Set aside 92 for Border 2.

    Make 48 blocks as shown with 3 green squares in one corner, 3 blue squares in the opposite corner, and the half-square triangle units down the center rotated as shown (green triangles on side with blue squares, blue triangles on side with green squares). Press.

    Arrange 4 blocks as shown, green corners at top left and bottom right, blue corners at top right and bottom left. Stitch into large block. Press. Make 12.

2. ASSEMBLE: Arrange large blocks as shown, green corners at top left and blue corners at top right. Stitch into horizontal rows. Stitch rows together. Press. See diagram on page 41.

3. BORDER 1: Make 2 side borders by piecing strips to same length as quilt. Stitch to quilt. Press. Repeat at top and bottom.

4. BORDER 2: Use 92 half-square triangle units from Step 1 to make borders as shown. Sides have 26 units; top and bottom have 20 units plus 2½" squares at each end (left from making blocks). Press. Stitch side borders to quilt. Press. Repeat at top and bottom.

5. BORDER 3: Repeat Step 3.

6. FINISH: Piece backing horizontally to same size as batting. Layer, baste, and quilt. Trim batting and backing even with quilt top. Bind quilt using ⅜" seam allowance.

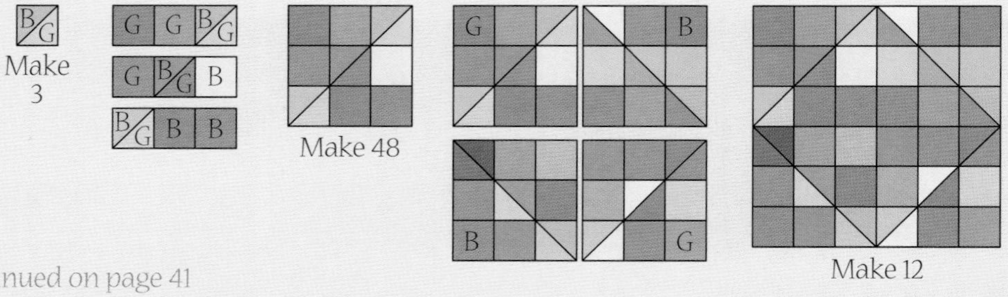

Continued on page 41

Stockings for Special People

★ Identify a theme for each stocking.

★ Choose fabrics in colors to match your theme.

★ Search your local hobby store for embellishments: diecut shapes, charms, glass beads, sewing notions, or fishing tackle. The scrapbooking/card-making section is full of "theme" ideas. Tack embellishments to ribbons at top of stocking.

New Baby
Tiny rubber ducky, teething ring, rattles, or small toys

Quilter
Tiny scissors, tape measure, spools of thread

Fisherman
Canvas, netting, lures and floats hung from heavy fishing line

---

1.   For each block:

Make 3

Make 48

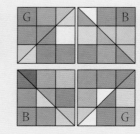
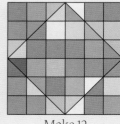
Make 12

Arctic Crystals, page 12. Stockings, pages 43-44. Gift Bags, page 8.

Cappuccino

Photo on page 15   Finished size approximately 60 x 78″   12″ & 6″ Blocks

Yardage Choose fabric with 42″ usable width.

Browns	⅜ yd each of 24 or more
Border	1 yd
Binding	⅔ yd
Backing	5 yd
Batting	66 x 84″

Cutting When 'strips' appears, cut selvage to selvage.

NOTE: Cut sets of pieces of the same fabric for each round. A set for the first round of Block A would be 2 pieces 6″ long & 2 pieces 8½″ long. **Cut and sew 1 block at a time.**

Browns	Block A	total of 15 squares 6″, 30 pieces 1¾ x 6″, 30 pieces 1¾ x 8½″ (Round 1), 30 pieces 2½ x 8½″, 30 pieces 2½ x 12½″ (Round 2)
	Block B	total of 24 squares 3½″, 48 pieces 1½ x 3½″, 48 pieces 1½ x 5½″ (Round 1), 48 pieces 1 x 5½″, 48 pieces 1 x 6½″ (Round 2)
	Block C	total of 24 squares 2½″, 48 pieces 2 x 2½″, 48 pieces 2 x 5½″ (Round 1), 48 pieces 1 x 5½″, 48 pieces 1 x 6½″ (Round 2)
Border		7-8 strips 3½″ wide
Binding		8 strips 2½″ wide

Directions Use ¼″ seam allowance unless otherwise noted.

1. BLOCKS: Using 1 fabric for each round, make blocks as shown. Press.

2. ASSEMBLE: Arrange blocks as shown. Stitch into horizontal rows. Stitch rows together. Press.

3. BORDER: Make 2 side borders by piecing strips to same length as quilt. Stitch to quilt. Press. Repeat at top and bottom.

4. FINISH: Piece backing vertically to same size as batting. Layer, baste, and quilt. Trim batting and backing even with quilt top. Bind quilt using ⅜″ seam allowance.

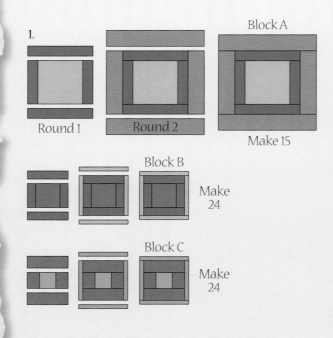

1.
Round 1   Round 2

Block A
Make 15

Block B
Make 24

Block C
Make 24

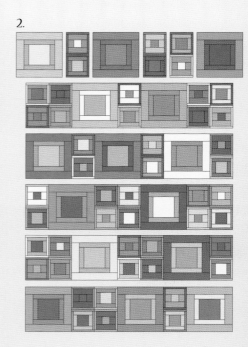

2.

Cappuccino Crisps

Enjoy these on frosty nights with a mug of mocha latte.

CAPPUCCINO CRISPS

½ c butter, softened
½ c brown sugar
½ t vanilla
¼ c whipping cream
⅛ c brewed coffee, very strong
⅓ c flour
¼ t salt
⅛ t baking soda
1 c quick rolled oats
1 c walnuts, chopped
6 oz chocolate chips

Preheat oven to 350°. Cream butter and sugar. Add vanilla, cream, and coffee. Combine flour, salt, and soda; blend into creamed mixture. Stir in oats and walnuts. Drop by teaspoon on greased cookie sheet. Bake 11 minutes, until edges are browned. When cool, drizzle with melted chocolate, then remove from cookie sheet.

Cappuccino, page 14.

Welcome Friends

Easy Centerpiece

★ Purchase pillar candles of different heights and widths

★ Glue cinnamon sticks and sprays of pepperberry to sides of candles.

★ Tie jute, cording, or ribbon around each candle.

★ Group candles on a pretty silver or glass tray, surround with evergreens, star garland, and miniature glass balls.

Photo on page 17.

Photo on page 17   Finished size approximately 36x12" (36x18" with mantle extension)

Yardage Choose fabric with 42" usable width.

Background	⅜ yd dark tan
Applique	¼ yd each light tan, medium green, dark green
	⅛ yd each light green, 2-4 reds, yellow (or yellow scrap)
Border	⅓ yd (¼ yd with mantle extension)
Optional mantle extension	⅜ yd - may want to use same fabric as triangles
Binding	⅜ yd
Backing	½ yd (¾ yd with mantle extension)
Batting	40x16" (40x22" with mantle extension)

Cutting When "strips" appears, cut selvage to selvage.

Background	1 piece 9x32½"
Applique	1 flower spray, 4 large flowers, 15 triangles, 1 set letters
	patterns on pages 50-54
Border	3 strips 2½" wide (2 strips 2½" wide with mantle extension)
Optional mantle extension	1 strip 8½" wide (or depth of mantle)
Binding	3-4 strips 2½" wide

Directions Use ¼" seam allowance unless otherwise noted.

1. APPLIQUE: Applique flowers, letters, and triangles. Triangles and stem of center flower extend into seam allowance.

2. BORDER: Cut 2 side borders to fit quilt. Stitch to quilt. Repeat at top and bottom—bottom only if extension is to be added. Press.

3. OPTIONAL MANTLE EXTENSION: Trim extension piece to width of hanging. Stitch to hanging. Press.

4. FINISH: Cut backing to same size as batting. Layer, baste, and quilt. Trim batting and backing even with quilt top. Bind quilt using ⅜" seam allowance.

Wall Hanging

Mantle Hanging

16

Two more wall/mantle hangings on pages 34-35.

Welcome Friends, page 16. Reversible Apron, page 36. Table Topper, page 36. Easy Centerpiece, page 16.

Tyrolean Christmas

The Christmas Spider

Long ago, a mother prepared for Christmas Eve by chasing all the spiders from the living room with a broom.

The spiders fled to the attic but crept downstairs later to see the Christmas tree. As they crawled along every branch, they were filled with joy as they admired the beauty of each ornament, but at the same time they draped the tree in their dusty cobwebs.

When the Christ Child came, he smiled at the sight of the happy spiders. He knew, however, that the mother would be heartbroken, so he touched the webs and turned them into sparkling silver, the first tinsel.

Photo on page 19   Finished size approximately 31x31"

Yardage
Choose fabric with 42" usable width.

Background	¼ yd each 6 creams
Applique	⅛ yd each 3 greens, 4 reds
Border 1	⅛ yd red
Border 2	¼ yd dark green
Corner triangles	½ yd green
Binding	⅜ yd
Backing	1¼ yd
Batting	35x35"

Cutting
When "strips" appears, cut selvage to selvage. *Cut these squares in **half** diagonally.

Background	creams - 24 squares 2" of each fabric, *2 squares 2⅜"
	red & green - *1 square each 2⅜"
Applique	4 large flowers, 4 tall flowers, 8 hearts, 32 triangles - patterns on page 54
Border 1	2 strips 1" wide
Border 2	2-3 strips 2" wide
Corner triangles	*2 squares 12⅞"
Binding	4 strips 2½" wide

Directions
Use ¼" seam allowance unless otherwise noted.

1. CENTER: Make 12 nine-patch blocks. Press. Make 4 center blocks as shown. Press. Stitch blocks into horizontal rows. Stitch rows together. Press.

2. BORDERS & CORNERS: Border 1 - Cut 2 side borders to fit quilt. Stitch to quilt. Repeat at top and bottom. Repeat for Border 2. Press. Corners - Stitch 1 triangle to each side, centered. Press.

3. APPLIQUE: Applique flowers, hearts, and triangles to quilt in positions shown below.

4. FINISH: Cut backing to same size as batting. Layer, baste, and quilt. Trim batting and backing even with quilt top. Bind quilt using ⅜" seam allowance.

1.

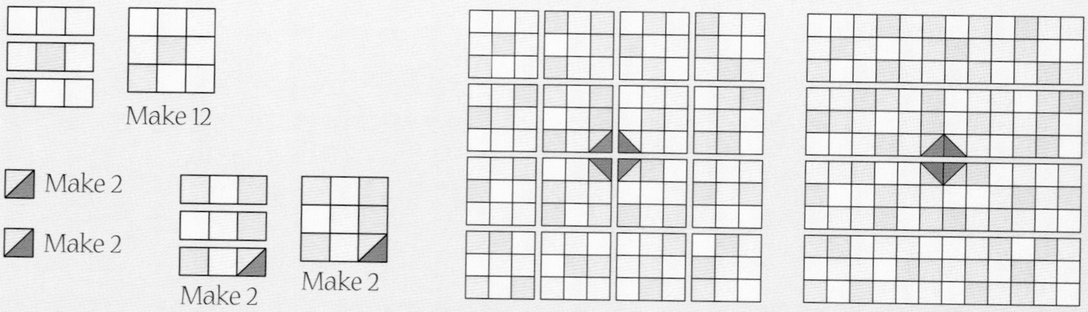

Make 12

◨ Make 2

◨ Make 2

 Make 2   Make 2

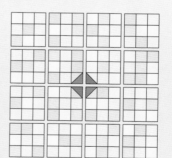

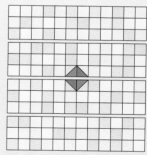

2.

3.

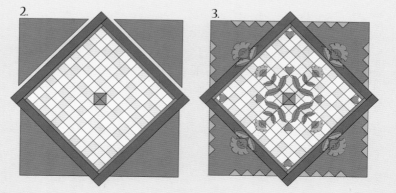

Tyrolean Christmas, page 18. Tyrolean Place Mats, page 37. Tyrolean Table Runner, page 37.

Deck the Halls

Tree Decorating

Invite friends and family to a tree decorating party! Make it more fun with hearty foods.

CHICKEN POSOLE

12-oz bag dried posole
6 c chicken stock
2-4 c water
1 med onion, diced
½ c each red & green pepper, diced
2 cloves garlic, minced
2 T butter
1 t each chili powder, cumin
½ t ground pepper
1 t salt
1 T dried chile caribe
15-oz can black beans
2 15-oz cans diced spicy tomatoes
3 c cooked, cubed chicken

Simmer posole in stock and water 4 hours, or until tender. Saute onions, peppers, and garlic in butter. Add to posole and stock. Add all spices, beans, and tomatoes. Simmer 1 hour. Add chicken and simmer 15 minutes. Serve with a dollop of sour cream or guacamole and tortilla chips.

Photo on page 21   Finished size approximately 50x62"   12" Block (with sashing)

Yardage Choose fabric with 42" usable width.

Background, sashing	1 yd black
Sashing, applique	¼ yd black/white lengthwise stripe
	⅜ yd each 1 green, 2 pinks, 2 yellows, 2 oranges, 2 reds, 2 purples, 2 blues
	⅜ yd pink for border ribbons
Border 1, 2	½ yd purple
Borders 2, 3	1⅛ yd black, ⅓ yd each pink & orange
Border 4	½ yd black/white lengthwise stripe
Binding	⅝ yd
Backing	3⅜ yd
Batting	56x68"

Cutting When "strips" appears, cut selvage to selvage. *Cut these squares in **half** diagonally.

Background, sashing	12 squares 9½", 12 squares 1½" (centers of horizontal sashing units)
Sashing	stripe - 12 pieces 1½x9½" - centers of vertical units
	others - cut a total of 24 pieces 1½x9½" **in pairs** -sides of vertical units
	cut a total of 12 pieces 1x12½" - tops of horizontal units
	cut a total of 12 pieces 2x12½" - bottoms of horizontal units
	for centers of horizontal units, cut the following **in pairs**: total of 12 pieces 1½x10½", total of 12 squares 1½"
Applique	3 round & 2 pointed ornaments, 6 small stars for each round ornament, 4 large stars & spirals, 3 hearts & 9 holly leaves, 7 hangers, 4 border ribbons - patterns on pages 45, 51, 53, 55, 56, 57
Border 1, 2	5 strips 1½" wide, *2 squares 2⅞"
Border 2	black - *44 squares 2⅞", 4 squares 2½"
	pink & orange - *21 squares 2⅞" each
Border 3	black - 6 strips 3½" wide
Border 4	6 strips 1¾" wide
Binding	6-7 strips 2½" wide

Directions Use ¼" seam allowance unless otherwise noted.

1. BLOCKS: Make 12 vertical sashing units with a pair of colored pieces on either side of a stripe piece. Press. Make 12 horizontal sashing units as shown using remaining sashing pieces. Make some with mostly warm colors and some with mostly cool colors, if desired. Press. Stitch vertical units to left sides of background squares. Press. Stitch horizontal units to bottoms of background squares. Press. Applique ornaments to blocks.

2. ASSEMBLE: Arrange blocks as shown. Stitch into horizontal rows. Stitch rows together. Press.

3. BORDER 1: Make 2 side borders by piecing strips to same length as quilt. Stitch to quilt. Press. Repeat at top and bottom.

4. BORDER 2: Make 42 half-square triangle units with black and orange. Make 42 half-square triangle units with black and

1.

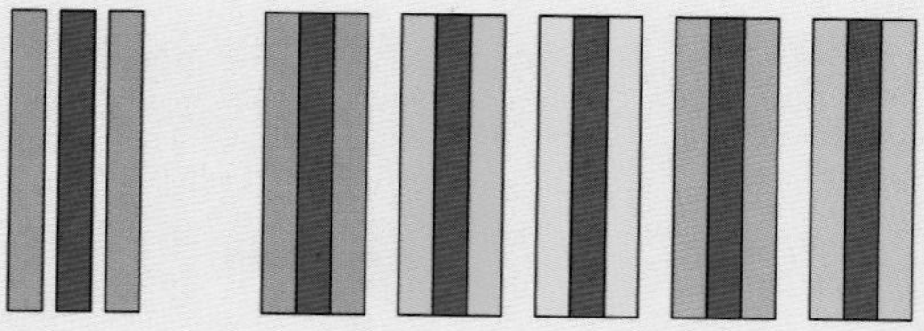

Make 12

Continued on page 38

Deck the Halls, page 20. Deck the Halls Tree Skirt, page 39. Deck the Halls Pillows, page 38.

Christmas Pickle

The Christmas Pickle

The tradition of the blown glass Christmas pickle ornament began many years ago in Laschau, Germany. The lucky child who finds the pickle ornament on the tree on Christmas morning receives an extra gift from St. Nicholas.

If the family cannot afford the extra gift, the pickle finder is rewarded by being the first to open their presents.

Production of this blown glass ornament began in the 1890s and is a fun tradition to continue into the twenty-first century!

Photo on page 23   Finished size approximately 59 x 83"   12" Blocks

Note: We love to make scrap quilts! When it comes time to give yardage in our books, we try to make sure enough fabrics are listed to create the scrappy look of the original without making buying the yardage unreasonable. One great way to expand your fabric collection is to have an exchange with friends.

Yardage Choose fabric with 42" usable width.

Greens	½ yd each of 24 or more - lights, mediums, & darks
Reds, purples, fuchsias	⅓ yd each of 4 or more
Border 1	½ yd
Border 2	1⅜ yd
Binding	⅔ yd
Backing	5⅓ yd
Batting	65 x 89"

Cutting When 'strips' appears, cut selvage to selvage. *Cut these squares in **half** diagonally.

Unit A	for each unit - *2 squares each of 2 greens 2⅞"
Unit B	make 24 copies of pattern piece D, page 47, for paper piecing
	for each unit, cut 1 set of pieces from patterns A-F (except D), pages 47 & 48,
	including 2-3 pieces (A, B, C, &/or E) from reds, purples, fuchsias
Border 1	7 strips 1¾" wide
Border 2	8 strips 5" wide
Binding	8 strips 2½" wide

Directions Use ¼" seam allowance unless otherwise noted.

1. UNIT A: Make 120 units using 2 fabrics in each. See diagram. Press.

2. UNIT B: For each unit, paper piece one D, using 2 greens. Stitch A through F together, matching center marks and outside edges of pieces. Make 24. Press.

3. BLOCKS: Arrange 5 Unit A and 1 Unit B as shown on page 42. Stitch into horizontal rows. Stitch rows together. Press.

4. ASSEMBLE: Arrange blocks, rotated as shown, and stitch into horizontal rows. Stitch rows together. Press.

5. BORDERS: Border 1 - Make 2 side borders by piecing strips to same length as quilt. Stitch to quilt. Press. Repeat at top and bottom. Repeat for Border 2.

6. FINISH: Piece backing vertically to same size as batting. Layer, baste, and quilt. Trim batting and backing even with quilt top. Bind quilt using ⅜" seam allowance.

1. Unit A

Make 4 for each unit

Make 120 units

2. Unit B

Make 1 for each unit

Make 24 units

Continued on page 42

Christmas Pickle, page 22.

Sugarplums

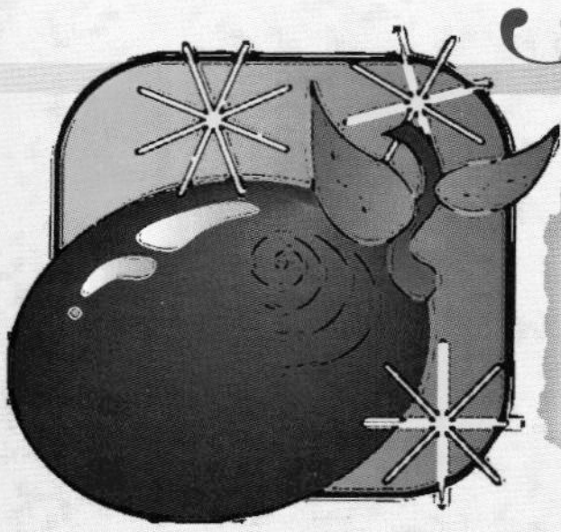

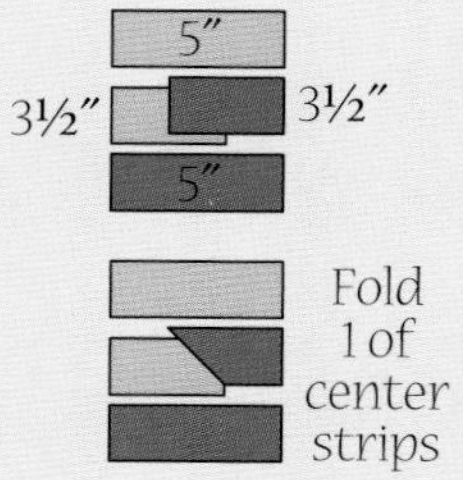

Holiday "Crackers"

★ Collect empty toilet paper tubes. Lightly coat outside with adhesive spray.

★ Fill tubes with little treasures like wrapped candy, confetti, miniature ornaments, and foil-wrapped chocolate coins.

★ Cut 7x12" pieces of wrapping paper or several layers of colored tissue paper using pinking shears. Roll around goodie-filled tube.

★ Tie ends with cord, ribbon, or jute.

★ Decorate with stickers.

For a dressier alternative, use coordinated fabrics instead of paper

Photo on page 25   Finished size approximately 57x66"   9" Block

Yardage Choose fabric with 42" usable width.

Blocks, Border 1	¼ yd each of 20 fabrics - plums
	OR 1 roll of 20 strips 6½" wide
Blocks	¼ yd each of 3 golds
Blocks - around edge	⅝ yd gold
Border 2	1¼ yd
Flat piping	½ yd
Binding	⅝ yd
Backing	3¾ yd
Batting	63x72"

Cutting When 'strips' appears, cut selvage to selvage.

Blocks, Border 1   3 strips 2" wide from each plum fabric
     cut 1 strip of each into 5" segments, cut 1 strip of each into 3½" segments
     3 strips 2" wide from each of 3 golds (¼-yd pieces)
     cut 1 strip of each into 5" segments, cut 1 strip of each into 3½" segments
     9 strips 2" wide from 'around edge' gold (⅝-yd piece)
     cut 5 strips into 5" segments, cut 4 strips into 3½" segments

Border 2	7 strips 5" wide
Flat piping	7 strips 1¾" wide
Binding	7 strips 2½" wide

Directions Use ¼" seam allowance unless otherwise noted.

1. LAYOUT: For each quarter-block, choose 2 colors and place 4 pieces as shown, folding back one of 3½" pieces in center at a 45° angle to simulate finished quarter block. Place pieces for **entire quilt** on floor or design wall, grouping and rotating as shown, and making sugarplums of the same fabric where corners of blocks meet. Cut remaining strips into 5" and 3½" segments as needed while working with color placement. Place pieces for a total of 30 blocks set 5x6. Place gold pieces cut from ⅝-yd piece around edge. See stars on diagram on page 42.

2. STITCH UNITS & BLOCKS: Pick up 1 quarter block at a time and stitch as shown, page 42. Press. Replace in position before moving on to next quarter block. Pick up four quarter blocks at a time and stitch into blocks. Press. Replace before moving on to next block. Make 30 blocks.

3. ASSEMBLE BLOCKS: Stitch blocks into horizontal rows as shown. Stitch rows together. Press.

4. BORDER 1: Cut remaining plum strips into 5" segments. Stitch segments into borders to fit each side of quilt. Stitch to sides of quilt. Press. Repeat at top and bottom.

5. BORDER 2: Make 2 side borders by piecing strips to same length as quilt. Stitch to quilt. Press. Repeat at top and bottom.

6. FINISH: Piece backing horizontally to same size as batting. Layer, baste, and quilt. Trim batting and backing even with quilt top.

   Stitch flat piping strips end to end. Press in half lengthwise. Cut 2 pieces to fit sides of quilt. Baste to sides of quilt, raw edges even. Repeat at top and bottom.

   Bind quilt using ⅜" seam allowance.

1.
For each quarter block:

5"
3½" 3½"
5"

Fold 1 of center strips

Continued on page 42

Sugarplums, page 24.

Tree of Life

Photo on page 27   Finished size approximately 46 x 33"   13½" & 6" Blocks

Historical Origins

The Tree of Life quilt pattern is thought to have originated in a motif by the same name that was frequently found in the Oriental rugs imported from India and Persia to eastern Atlantic seaports.

These rugs graced eighteenth-century homes in the colonies and became popular not only for their intrinsic beauty but also because they evoked faith and belief in eternal life.

Thus the design soon became a favored one among the religiously inclined settlers of the colonies. The appeal of this ancient design has enjoyed continued popularity in quilting.

Yardage
Choose fabric with 42" usable width.

Tree block, sawtooth border corners	¼ yd blue, ⅛ yd light green, ¼ yd dark green, ¼ yd each 2 medium greens; ⅙ yd brown
Narrow tree block border	⅛ yd light teal
Sawtooth border	¼ yd each 1 black, 1 red
Applique background	⅓ yd blue, ¼ yd light teal, ⅜ yd black
Applique	¼ yd each 2 reds, 2 greens; ⅛ yd light brown
Narrow framing borders	¼ yd red
Small block sashing	⅛ yd green
Star blocks	¼ yd each 3 reds, 2 greens
Outer border	½ yd blue
Tabs	½ yd dark teal
Binding	½ yd
Backing	1⅝ yd
Batting	50 x 37"

Cutting
When "strips" appears, cut selvage to selvage. *Cut these squares in **half** diagonally.

Tree block	*1 blue square 6⅞" (a), *1 blue square 3⅞" (b), *1 blue square 5⅜" (c), 2 blue pieces 3½ x 6½"
	3 light green squares 2"
	*15 dark green squares 2⅜"
	*18 medium green #1 squares 2⅜"
	*1 medium green #2 square 6⅞"
	1 brown square 3⅞"
	cut 1½ x 6⅞" trunk from brown fabric backed with fusible web
Sawtooth border corners	4 squares blue 2"
Narrow tree block border	2 strips 1¼"
Sawtooth border	*20 black & *20 red squares 2⅜"
Applique background	2 strips blue 4¼" wide, 4 strips teal 1½" wide, 4 strips black 2½" wide
Applique	1 heart, 4 flowers - patterns on page 50
Narrow framing borders	5 strips 1¼" wide
Small block sashing	6 pieces 1½ x 6½"
Star blocks	*32 red #1 squares 2⅜" - points
	*32 green #1 squares 2⅜" - background
	16 red #2 squares 2" - center
	16 red #3 squares 2" - center
	32 green #2 squares 2" - corners
Outer border	4 strips 3½" wide
Tabs	7 pieces 6½ x 8"
Binding	5 strips 2½" wide

Directions
Use ¼" seam allowance unless otherwise noted.

1. TREE BLOCK: Make center block following diagrams on page 40. Applique trunk before stitching large and small triangles to lower part of tree block. Press. Applique heart to triangle above trunk when block is finished.

Continued on page 40

Tree of Life, page 26.

Snowbuddy

Continued from page 2

Directions Use ¼" seam allowance unless otherwise noted.

1. LARGE TREE ROW: Make 6 large tree blocks as shown. Trim seam allowances to ¼" after stitching diagonal seams. Numbers on diagrams indicate cut sizes of each piece. Press. Stitch into 2 horizontal rows of 3 blocks. Stitch a dark red border to top of one row and bottom of other row. Press.

2. SMALL TREE ROWS: Using paper piecing pattern on page 59, make 8 small tree blocks. Press. Stitch into 2 vertical rows of 4 blocks each. Press.

3. HOUSE ROW: Make 2 house blocks as shown. Press. Stitch 1¼ x 9½" dark red sashing piece between house blocks as shown. Stitch remaining 9½" sashing pieces to sides, then 23" sashing pieces to top and bottom. Press.

4. CHECKERBOARD BORDERS: Make 3 strip sets as shown. Press. Crosscut into 2⅜" segments. Stitch 21 segments together as shown. Make 2. Press.

5. ASSEMBLE:

   Center Panel: Stitch small tree block rows to sides of upper snowman background. Stitch lower snowman background pieces to bottom in any order desired. Add green borders then narrow dark red border at top as shown. Press.

   Stitch house row to bottom of center panel. Press.

   Stitch checkerboard border units to each side. Press.

   Stitch tree units to top and bottom Press.

6. APPLIQUE: Make a strip set 13 strips wide with white strips. Press. Apply fusible web to wrong side. Cut out 12", 9", and 6" circles for snowman body. Applique center panel using photo as a guide for placement.

7. LAYER & QUILT: Cut backing to same size as batting. Layer, baste, and quilt. Trim batting and backing even with quilt top. Stitch buttons to snowman.

8. PRAIRIE POINTS: Press squares in half diagonally, then in half again diagonally. Pin to top and bottom, points inward as shown, tucking into each other to make fit. Baste to quilt with a scant ¼" seam allowance.

9. FACING: Cut facing strips to fit top and bottom of quilt. Press in half lengthwise, wrong sides together. Stitch to top and bottom, right sides together. Turn to back of quilt. Prairie points will extend from edge. Hand stitch folded edge of facing to back of quilt. Repeat at sides, tucking in raw ends at each corner.

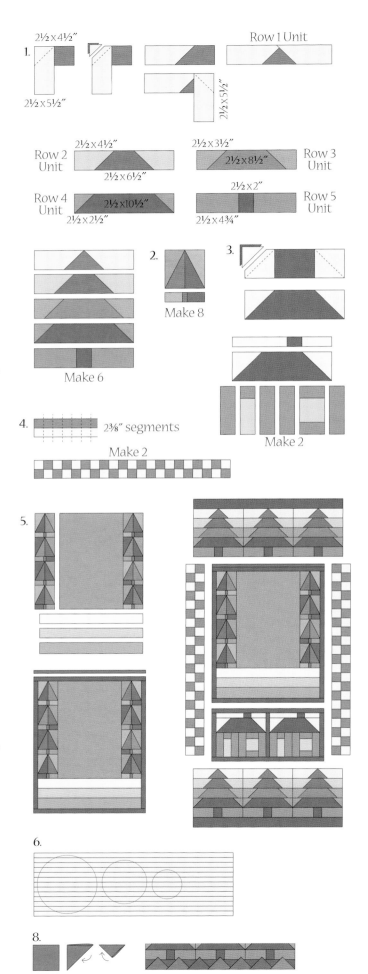

Snow Buddy Tree Skirt

Photo on page 3   Finished diameter 48"

Yardage Choose fabric with 42" usable width.

Tan	½ yd - background
Dark green	¾ yd - center, center binding
Medium greens	½ yd each of 2 - triangles
Dark reds	¾ yd each of 2 - triangles, prairie points
Backing	3¼ yd - includes facing
Batting	54 x 54"

Cutting

Tan	6 & 6 reversed, using pattern, page 58
Dark green	1 piece 2¼ x18" on bias
	6 & 6 reversed, using pattern
Medium greens	3 & 3 reversed each, using pattern
Dark reds	3 & 3 reversed each, using pattern
	21 squares each - 4¼"
Facing	2 pieces 2½" wide x **length** of fabric - set aside remaining fabric for backing, Step 4

Directions Use ¼" seam allowance unless otherwise noted.

1. UNIT 1: Stitch dark green triangles together—1 and 1 reversed—to make 6 large triangles. Press.

   UNIT 2: Stitch medium red triangles together—1 and 1 reversed of the same fabric—to make 3 large triangles. Repeat with other medium red triangles. Press.

   UNIT 3: Stitch medium green and tan triangles together as shown. Make 3 of each. Press.

2. SECTIONS: Arrange units on table or floor as shown. Stitch units into 6 sections—3 of Section A and 3 of Section B. Press.

3. ASSEMBLE: Stitch sections together. Stop stitching approximately 2" from center as this area will be cut away for tree trunk. Press.

4. LAYER & QUILT: Piece backing to same size as batting. Layer backing, batting, and tree skirt. Baste. Quilt. Trim batting and backing even with quilt top. Mark 6" circle at center. Beginning at outer edge, straight stitch ⅛" from seam, around center marking, and back out to edge. See diagram on page 30. Cut between stitching lines and close to stitched circle.

5. PRAIRIE POINTS: Press squares in half diagonally, then in half again diagonally. Pin 7 prairie points to each outside edge of tree skirt, points inward as shown, tucking into

each other to make fit. Do not overlap at corners. Baste prairie points to tree skirt with a scant ¼" seam allowance.

6. FACING: Stitch facing strips end to end. Press in half lengthwise, wrong sides together. Cut 2 pieces the length of back opening plus 2". Stitch facing, right sides together, to each side of tree skirt at center back opening. Turn facing to back of tree skirt and hand stitch folded edge down. Trim ends of facing even with tree skirt. Leaving a ½" extension at beginning and end, stitch facing to outside edge of tree skirt, right sides together. Pivot at each corner; do not create a tuck. Turn facing to back of tree skirt; prairie points extend from edge. Hand stitch folded edge of facing to back of tree skirt, mitering angles and tucking in extensions at center back opening.

7. BIND CENTER: Press dark green bias piece in half lengthwise, wrong sides together. Bind center hole using ¼" seam allowance.

1.

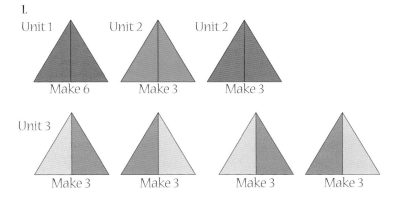

Unit 1   Make 6
Unit 2   Make 3
Unit 2   Make 3
Unit 3   Make 3   Make 3   Make 3   Make 3

2-3.

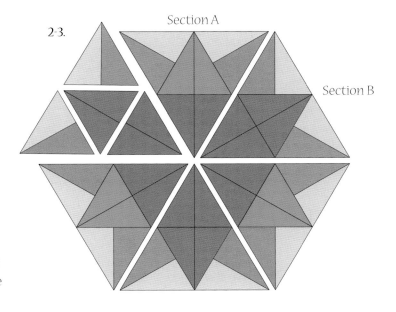

Section A

Section B

Continued on page 30

Snow Buddy Tree Skirt

Continued from page 29

4.

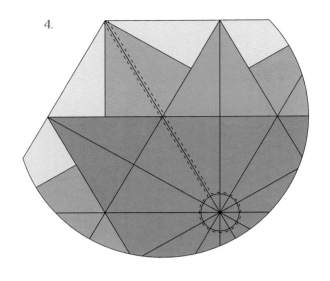

5.

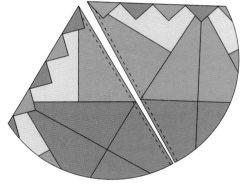

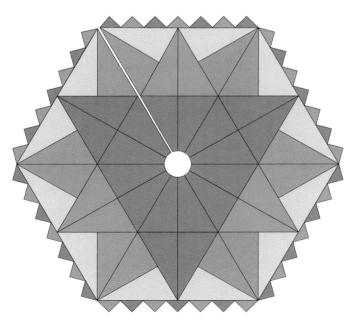

Snow Buddy Pillows

Photo on page 3   Finished size 16"

Materials   Choose fabric with 42" usable width.

ALL PILLOWS For each pillow

Border 1	⅛ yd
Border 2	¼ yd
Backing for quilting	⅝ yd
Envelope backing	⅝ yd
Batting	18×18"
Binding	¼ yd
Buttons	4 large, 4 small
Pillow form	16"

TREE For 1 pillow

Backgrounds	scraps or ⅛ yd each of 5
Trees	scraps or ⅛ yd each of 4
Trunk	scrap or ⅛ yd

SNOWMAN For 1 pillow

Background	⅓ yd
Applique	scraps or ⅛ yd each, including 4-7 whites for strip-pieced head
Black buttons	2 medium for eyes, 5 tiny for mouth

HOUSE For 1 pillow

Background, roof/chimney	scraps or ⅙ yd each
"Siding", door/window, grass	scraps or ⅛ yd each

Cutting   When "strips" appears, cut selvage to selvage.

ALL PILLOWS For each pillow

Border 1	2 pieces 1½×10½", 2 pieces 1½×12½"
Border 2	2 pieces 2½×12½", 2 pieces 2½×16½"
Envelope backing	2 pieces 16½×20"
Binding	2 strips 3¼" wide

TREE For 1 pillow

Background	2 pieces each: Row 1, top - 2½×5½"; Row 2 - 2½×4½"; Row 3 - 2½×3½"; Row 4 - 2½×2½"; Row 5 - 2½×4¾"
Tree	1 piece each: Row 1, top - 2½×4½"; Row 2 - 2½×6½"; Row 3 - 2½×8½"; Row 4 - 2½×10½"
Trunk	Row 5 - 2½×2"

SNOWMAN For 1 pillow

Background	1 square 10½"
Head	8 pieces 1½×8"
Applique	patterns on page 60

HOUSE For 1 pillow

Background	2 squares 3½", 1 piece 1½×6", 1 piece 1½×3½"
Roof, chimney	1 piece 3½×10½", 1 piece 1½×2"

Siding	4 pieces 2×5½″, 2 pieces 1¾×3″,
	1 piece 1¾×2″
Door, window	1 piece 2×4¼″, 1 square 3″
Grass	1 piece 1½×10½″

Directions Use ¼″ seam allowance unless otherwise noted.

TREE

Make one tree block using diagrams for Step 1 on page 28. Press. Go to All Pillows section.

SNOWMAN

For head, stitch white pieces together side to side. Press. Apply fusible web to wrong side. Cut out 6″ circle. Applique block, keeping pieces out of seam allowance. Go to All Pillows section. After quilting, stitch buttons to head.

HOUSE

Make one house block using diagrams for Step 3 on page 28. Add grass piece to bottom. Press. Go to All Pillows section.

ALL PILLOWS

1. BORDERS: Stitch short Border 1 pieces to sides of block, then long Border 1 pieces to top and bottom. Press. Repeat for Border 2.

2. QUILT: Cut quilting backing to same size as batting. Layer and quilt as desired. Trim batting and backing to same size as pillow top.

3. ENVELOPE BACK: With wrong sides together, press both envelope backing pieces in half, to 16½×10″. Place backing pieces on wrong side of pillow top, raw edges matching, folded edges overlapping at center of pillow. Stitch around outside edge a scant ½″ from edge. Test fit by trying pillow cover on pillow form. Adjust if necessary and trim seam allowance to ½″.

4. BINDING: Stitch binding strips together end to end. Press in half lengthwise, wrong sides together. Bind pillow using ½″ seam allowance.

5. BUTTONS: Stack small buttons on large buttons and stitch to each corner of Border 2.

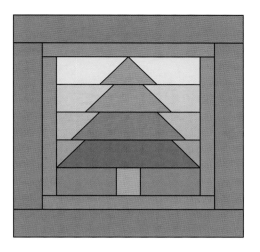

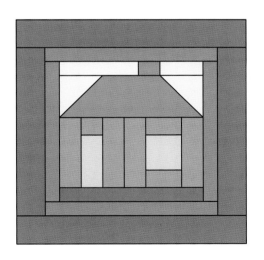

Starry Starry Night

Continued from page 6

3.

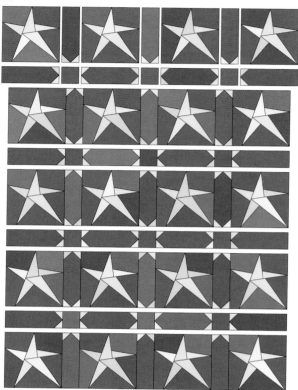

5.  Make 72

Sides - Make 2

Top and bottom - Make 2

Strippy Trees

Continued from page 8

2. ASSEMBLE: Arrange blocks as shown. Stitch blocks into horizontal rows. Stitch rows together. Press.

3. BORDER 1: Make 2 side borders by piecing strips to same length as quilt. Stitch to quilt. Press. Repeat at top and bottom.

4. BORDER 2: Repeat Step 3.

5. FINISH: Piece backing horizontally to same size as batting. Layer, baste, and quilt. Trim batting and backing even with quilt top. Bind quilt using 3/8" seam allowance.

2.

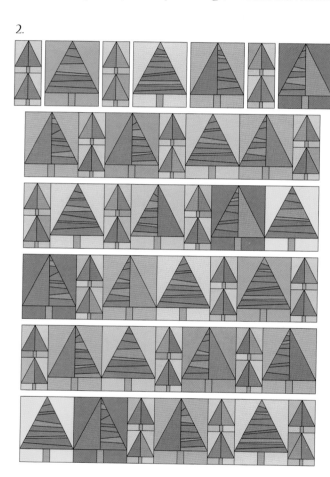

Kaleidoscope

Continued from page 10

2. ASSEMBLE: Arrange blocks and black setting triangles as shown. Stitch into diagonal units. Stitch into horizontal rows. Stitch rows together. Press.

3. BORDERS: Border 1 - Make 2 side borders by piecing strips to same length as quilt. Stitch to quilt. Press. Repeat at top and bottom. Repeat for Borders 2 and 3.

4. FINISH: Piece backing horizontally to same size as batting. Layer, baste, and quilt. Trim batting and backing even with quilt top. Bind quilt using 3⁄8″ seam allowance.

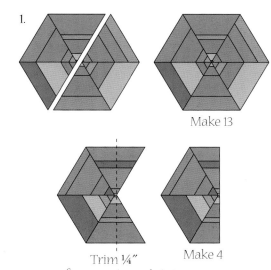

1.

Make 13

Trim ¼″
from center point

Make 4

2.

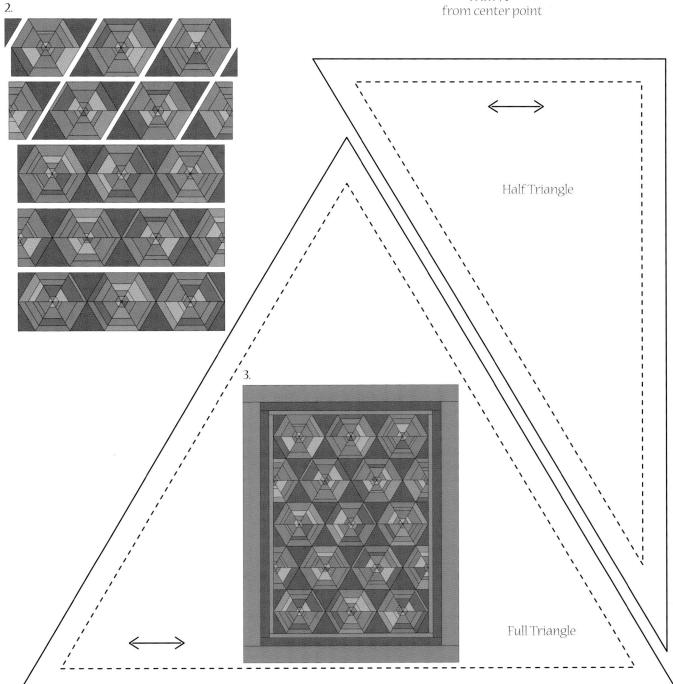

3.

Half Triangle

Full Triangle

Strippy Trees Hanging

Finished size 32x16" (32x24" with mantle extension)

See diagram on page 16 and photo on page 17 for mantle extension option.

Yardage   Choose fabric with 42" usable width.

Trees	¼ yd each of 5 greens
	⅛ yd each of 2 pinks
Backgrounds	¼ yd each of 3 blues
Trunks	scrap or ⅛ yd brown
Sashing	¼ yd dark blue
Border	¼ yd dark green
Stars	scraps or ⅛ yd pieces of 2-3 yellows
Opt. mantle extension	⅜ yd
Binding	⅓ yd
Backing	⅝ yd (⅞ yd with mantle ext.)
Binding	⅜ yd
Batting	36x20" (36x28" with mantle ext.)

Cutting   When "strips" appears, cut selvage to selvage.

Trees	greens - 3 pieces 5x9", then see Step 1 of Directions
Backgrounds	2 pieces 2½x4" of each blue fabric - trunk units
Trunks	3 pieces 1½x2½"
Applique	6 stars - pattern on page 55
Sashing	4 pieces 1½x10½", 2 pieces 1½x28½"
Border	3 strips 2½"
Opt. mantle ext.	1 strip 8½" wide (or depth of mantle)
Binding	3-4 strips 2½" (4 strips with extension)

Directions   Use ¼" seam allowance unless otherwise noted.

1. BLOCKS: Make 1 copy each of patterns on pages 45 and 46. Tape halves together. Make 3 copies of full-sized pattern. Trace diagonal and center vertical tree lines to wrong sides of patterns. Cut strips from tree fabrics 1-2½" wide in increments of ¼". String piece right half of tree top unit. To finish, see directions and diagrams for Block C on page 8. Press. Applique 2 stars to each block, keeping them out of seam allowance. Make 3 blocks.

2. ASSEMBLE: Stitch short sashing pieces and blocks together. Stitch long sashing pieces to top and bottom. Press.

3. BORDER: Cut 2 side borders the same length as quilt. Stitch to quilt. Repeat at top and bottom. Press.

4. OPTIONAL MANTLE EXTENSION: Trim extension piece to width of panel. Stitch to top of panel. Press.

5. FINISH: Cut backing to same size as batting. Layer, baste, and quilt. Trim batting and backing even with quilt top. Bind quilt using ⅜" seam allowance.

1.
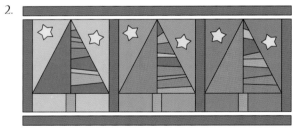

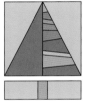
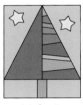

String piece on traced side of paper pattern

Make 3

2.

House & Trees Hanging

Finished size 37x13″ (37x21″ with mantle extension)

See diagram on page 16 and photo on page 17 for mantle extension option.

Yardage
Choose fabric with 42″ usable width.

House	⅛ yd each cream, red, tan, yellow, green
	scrap or ⅛ yd red - chimney
Trees	⅛ yd each of 4 greens
	⅛ yd each of 5 tans
Trunks, border	¼ yd brown
Sashing	⅛ yd each green, cream
Opt. mantle extension	⅜ yd
Binding	⅜ yd
Backing	⅝ yd (¾ yd with mantle extension)
Batting	41x17″ (41x25″ with mantle ext.)

Cutting
When "strips" appears, cut selvage to selvage.

House	cream: 2 squares 3½″, 1 piece 1½x6″, 1 piece 1½x3½″
	red: 1 piece 3½x10½″ - roof
	red: 1 piece 1½x2″ - chimney
	tan: 4 pieces 2x5½″, 1 piece 1¾x2″, 2 pieces 1¾x3″
	yellow: 1 piece 2x4¼″, 1 square 3″
	green: 1 piece 1½x10½″
Trees	1 strip 2½″ of each green & each tan
Trunks, border	2 pieces 2x2½″, 3 strips 2″
Sashing	20 squares 1½″ of each fabric
Opt. mantle ext.	1 strip 8½″ wide (or depth of mantle)
Binding	3-4 strips 2½″ (4 strips with extension)

Directions
Use ¼″ seam allowance unless otherwise noted.

1. BLOCKS: Make 1 house block and 2 tree blocks using diagrams on page 28. Stitch green piece to bottom of house block. For tree block, cut 2½″ strips into sizes shown on diagrams and use each tan in a different row on the 2 tree blocks. Press.

2. SASHING: Stitch green and cream squares together as shown. Make 2. Press.

3. ASSEMBLE: Stitch sashing and blocks together. Press.

4. BORDER: Cut 2 side borders the same length as quilt. Stitch to quilt. Repeat at top and bottom. Press.

5. OPTIONAL MANTLE EXTENSION: Trim extension piece to width of panel. Stitch to top of panel. Press.

6. FINISH: Cut backing to same size as batting. Layer, baste, and quilt. Trim batting and backing even with quilt top. Bind quilt using ⅜″ seam allowance.

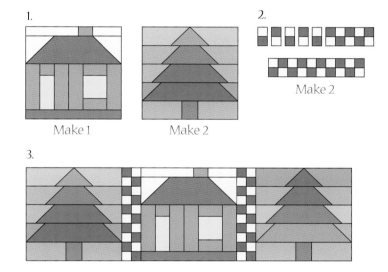

1.

Make 1   Make 2

2.

Make 2

3.

Reversible Apron

Photo on page 17

Yardage Choose fabric with 42" usable width.

Apron	1 yd each of 2 fabrics
Pockets	¼ yd
Applique	scraps or ⅛ yd pieces

Cutting When "strips" appears, cut selvage to selvage.

Apron	1 from each fabric - pattern on page 54
Ties	3 strips 1½" from each fabric
Pockets	2 pieces 6½ x 12½"
Applique	2 tall flowers - pattern on page 54

Directions Use ¼" seam allowance unless otherwise noted.

1. POCKETS: Fold each pocket piece in half crosswise, to 6½ x 6¼", right sides together. Stitch around pockets, leaving openings on sides for turning. Clip corners, turn right side out, and press. Applique pockets–shorten stem to base of leaves. Pin pockets to right sides of apron pieces, folded edges of pockets placed 4" down from top edges and centered from left to right. Topstitch side and bottom edges of pockets.

2. TIES: Separate ties into 3 pairs, 1 strip of each fabric in each pair. Set 1 pair aside for neck. To make 2 waist ties, place pieces of each pair right sides together and stitch both long sides and one short end. Clip corners. Turn right side out using eraser end of a pencil, dowel, or turning tool. Press. Pin unfinished ends of waist ties between marks on sides of apron, right sides together, raw edges even. To make neck ties, cut pieces in half lengthwise, to 1½ x 22". Repeat stitching and turning directions. Pin unfinished ends between marks on top edge of apron.

3. FINISH: Place apron pieces right sides together. Pin unfinished tie ends to apron to keep them out of seams. Stitch around apron, catching raw ends of ties in seam and leaving an opening on one side for turning. Clip corners, turn right side out, and press. Slipstitch opening closed. Topstitch apron ¼" from edge.

Table Topper

Photo on page 17   Finished size approximately 48 x 48"

Yardage Choose fabric with 42" usable width.

Large print	1 yd	center
Green	¾ yd	Border 1, binding
Red	¾ yd	Borders 2, 4
Black	1½ yd	Borders 2, 3, 4
Backing	3¼ yd	
Batting	52 x 52"	

Cutting When "strips" appears, cut selvage to selvage.
*Cut these squares in **half** diagonally.

Large print	1 piece 30½ x 30½"
Green	2 pieces 1½ x 30½", 2 pieces 1½ x 32½"
	6 strips 2¼" wide - binding
Red	*76 squares 2⅞", 4 squares 2½"
Black	*76 squares 2⅞", 4 squares 2½",
	4 squares 4½", 4 pieces 4½ x 36½"

Directions Use ¼" seam allowance unless otherwise noted.

1. PIECED BORDERS: Make 152 red and black half-square triangles. Make Borders 2, 3, and 4 as shown, rotating half-square triangle units to create larger black and red triangles, and stitching squares to ends for top and bottom borders. Press.

2. ASSEMBLE: Stitch short Border 1 pieces to sides of center panel. Stitch long pieces to top and bottom. Press. Repeat stitching order for Borders 2, 3, and 4. Note direction of black and red triangles on whole-quilt diagram on page 48. Press.

3. FINISH: Piece backing to same size as batting. Layer backing, batting, and top. Baste. Quilt. Trim batting and backing even with quilt top. Bind using ¼" seam allowance.

1.

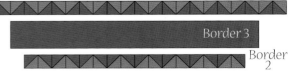

Make 152

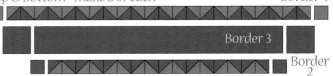

Continued on page 48

Tyrolean Table Runner

Photo on page 19   Finished size 12×42"

Yardage
Choose fabric with 42" usable width.

Background	⅜ yd each green, black
Squares	⅛ yd each light red, medium red
Applique	⅛ yd each 3 reds, 2 greens
Binding	⅓ yd
Backing	1⅜ yd
Batting	16×46"

Cutting
When "strips" appears, cut selvage to selvage.

Background	1 piece 9½×28½" - green
	2 pieces 2×28½", 2 pieces 5½×12½" - black
Squares	6 squares 2½" of each fabric
Applique	6 tall flowers - shorten stems to 2¾" - omit large leaves - patterns on page 54
Binding	3 strips 2½" wide

Directions
Use ¼" seam allowance unless otherwise noted.

1. APPLIQUE: Applique 3 flowers to each 5½×12½" black rectangle, extending stem but not leaves into seam allowance.

2. ASSEMBLE: Stitch long black pieces to green piece. Stitch short black pieces to each end, stems flowers facing as shown. Press. Stitch red squares into 2 units of 6, alternating fabrics. Press. Stitch to ends of table runner. Press.

3. FINISH: Cut backing to same size as batting. Layer, baste, and quilt. Trim batting and backing even with quilt top. Bind table runner using ⅜" seam allowance.

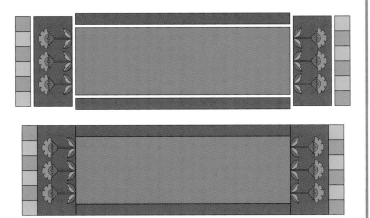

Tyrolean Place Mats

Photo on page 19   Finished size 14×18"   Makes 4

Yardage
Choose fabric with 42" usable width.

Prequilted fabric	1 yd
Applique	⅛ yd each of 2 reds
	¼ yd each of 2 greens
Binding	⅞ yd

Cutting
When "strips" appears, cut selvage to selvage.

Prequilted fabric	4 pieces 14×18"
Applique	8 tall flowers - shorten stems to 3¾" - patterns on page 54
Binding	8 strips 3¼" wide

Directions

1. APPLIQUE: Applique 2 flowers on right side of each place mat, keeping pieces ¾-1" from edge.

2. BIND: Stitch 2 binding strips together end to end. Press in half lengthwise, wrong sides together. Bind place mat with ½" seam allowance. Repeat for other place mats.

Deck the Halls

Continued from page 20

pink. Make 4 half-square triangle units with black and purple. Press. Stitch into borders as shown, plain black squares placed at center of each border. Press. Stitch side borders to quilt. Press. Repeat with top and bottom borders.

5. BORDER 3: Repeat Step 3. Applique ribbons to each border, centered side to side and end to end. Press. Repeat Step 2.

6. BORDER 4: Repeat Step 3.

7. FINISH: Piece backing horizontally to same size as batting. Layer, baste, and quilt. Trim batting and backing even with quilt top. Bind quilt using ⅜" seam allowance.

1.

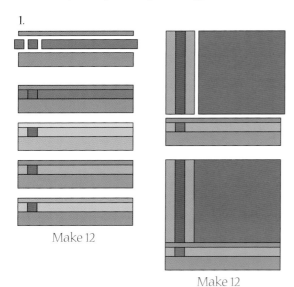

Make 12

Make 12

2.

4.
Make 1 - Right side

Make 1 - Left side

Make 2 - Top & bottom

Deck the Halls Pillows

Photo on page 21   Finished size 16"

Use colored leftovers from quilt for sashing, applique, borders, and binding, or purchase ⅜-yard pieces of several fabrics. Purchase ⅜ yard background fabric (will make 3 pillows), ⅝ yd for envelope back (for **each** pillow), 16" pillow forms, plus 18" squares of batting and backing for optional quilting of the pillow top(s).

Make blocks using cutting chart and directions for quilt on page 20. Add 2 borders with finished widths of ½" and 1½". Cut 2 binding strips 3¼" wide for each pillow. To finish, follow directions for all pillows on page 31, omitting buttons.

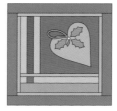

Deck the Halls Tree Skirt

Photo on page 21   Finished diameter 52″

Yardage Choose fabric with 42″ usable width.

Background	3⅓ yd
Appliques	⅛ yd each of 5 fabrics - outside edge
	½ yd - large stars
	⅙ yd - small stars on large stars
	⅓ yd - other small stars
Backing	3⅓ yd
Binding	⅞ yd
Batting	56 x 56″

Cutting

Appliques	32 triangles, 7 large stars, 7 small stars (on large stars), 12 other small stars, 7 spirals - patterns on pages 51, 56, 58
Binding	bias strips 2½″ wide, pieced to 245″ long

Directions Use ¼″ seam allowance unless otherwise noted.

1. PREPARE: Piece top to same size as batting. Fold top in quarters and mark center. Using a string compass, mark 52″ circle. Mark 6″ circle in center. Mark line for center back. See diagrams.

2. APPLIQUE: Scatter appliques using diagram as a guide. Overlap triangles at outside edge so that all 32 fit around circle—8 in each quarter-circle. Stitch appliques in place.

3. LAYER & QUILT: Piece backing to same size as batting. Layer backing, batting, and top. Baste. Quilt. Stitch close to pencil marks as shown. Cut on pencil marks.

4. BIND: Bind raw edges using ⅜″ seam allowance.

1.

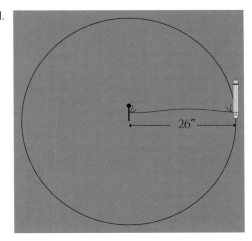

1.

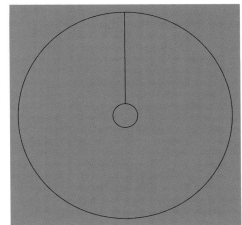

2.

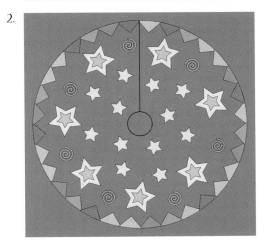

3.

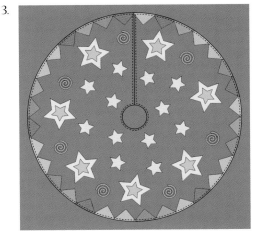

Tree of Life

Continued from page 26

2. STAR BLOCK UNITS: Make 8 blocks as shown below. Press. Referring to last diagram for Step 6, page 41, stitch into vertical rows of 4 blocks with 1½ x 6½" sashing pieces between blocks. Press. Cut 2 narrow framing border strips to same length as rows of blocks. Stitch framing strip to one side of each row of blocks.

3. SAWTOOTH BORDER: Make 40 half-square triangle units. Press. Stitch into 4 borders of 10 units reversing direction at center as shown. Stitch blue squares to ends of 2 of the borders. Press.

4. CORNER UNITS: Make 2 strip sets as shown with blue, light teal, and black strips. Press.
Make full-sized pattern below. Using pattern, cut 8 triangles as shown, gray lines of pattern placed along each side of teal strip. Stitch triangles together into 4 corner units. Press.

5. APPLIQUE: Applique flowers to corner units, extending stem into seam allowance.

6. ASSEMBLE: Assemble as shown. For outer border, cut strips to same length as quilt. Stitch to sides. Piece strips to same width as quilt and stitch to top and bottom of quilt. Press.

7. FINISH: Cut backing to same size as batting. Layer, baste, and quilt. Trim batting and backing even with quilt top.

Make 7 tabs: Fold tab pieces in half, to 3¼ x 8". Stitch 8" side. Turn right side out and fold in half, raw edges even. Baste to top of quilt on wrong side, raw edges even and approximately 3" apart.

Bind quilt using ⅜" seam allowance.

Diagrams continued on page 41

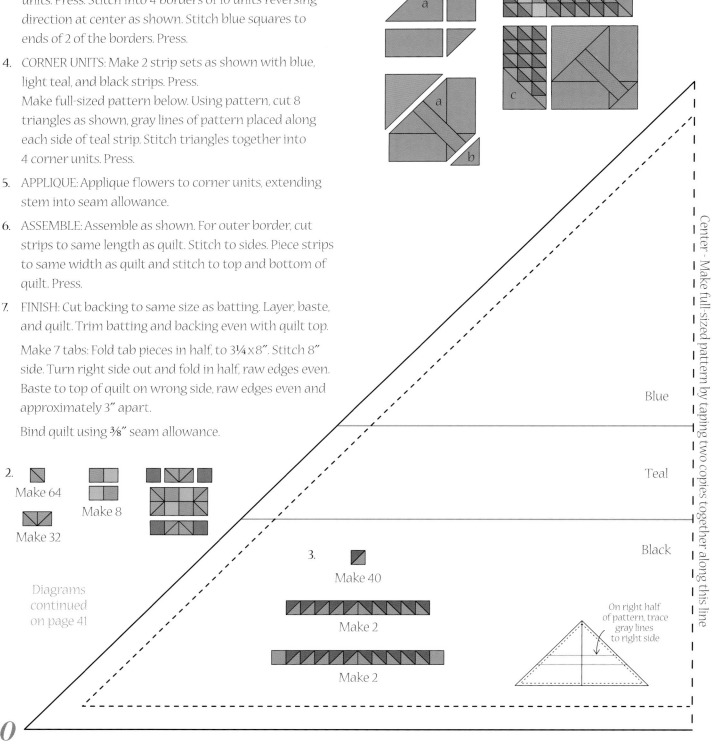

4.

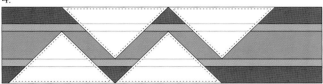

Make 2 strip sets. Cut 8 triangles matching gray lines on each side of teal strip.

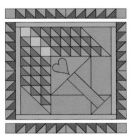

5.

Make 4

6.

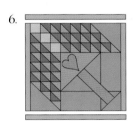

2.

4.

Sides - Make 2

Top & Bottom - Make 2

3.

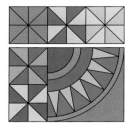

Make 24

4.

1. Lay out pieces for **entire quilt** (upper left shown here)

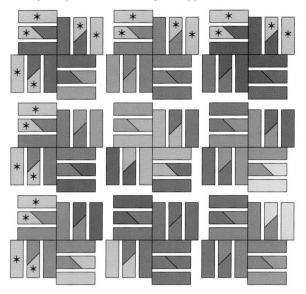

2.

Stitch, trim

Make 30

3.

Stockings Plain Background

Photos on pages 11, 13   Finished length 20"

Materials Choose fabric with 42" usable width.

Stocking	¾ yd
Cuff	⅜ yd
Lining	¾ yd
Appliques	large scraps or ¼ yd pieces
Binding	½ yd
Thin batting	2 pieces 15 x 24"
Charms	1-2 yd narrow ribbon, dye-cut wood shapes, miniature ornaments, beads, buttons, bells

Cutting

Stocking	2 pieces 15 x 24"
Cuff	1 square 10"
Appliques	as desired - patterns on pages 49-55
Lining	2 pieces 15 x 24"
Binding	bias strips 2½" wide, pieced to 80" long

Directions Use ¼" seam allowance unless otherwise noted.

1. FRONT: Layer lining wrong side up, batting, and stocking fabric right side up. Machine quilt as desired. Cut out stocking front with toe pointed the direction shown. Press cuff fabric in half wrong sides together. Open out and place right side down on stocking matching raw edges at top. Stitch along pressed line. Flip lower part over to right side and press. Trim even with sides of stocking. Pin, then baste cuff in place ¼" from edge. Applique stocking front using photos and diagrams as guides for placement. Reduce letters on a copier for longer names, and/or overlap edges of letters if necessary to make name fit.

2. BACK: Layer lining wrong side up, batting, then stocking fabric right side up. Machine quilt as desired. Cut out stocking back with toe pointed the direction shown.

3. BIND: Press binding in half lengthwise, wrong sides together. Bind top edges of stocking front and back using ⅜" seam allowance. Place stocking front on back with lining sides facing and baste ¼" from curved edge. Bind curved edge using ⅜" seam allowance; leave a 6" tail at top of heel side for making hanger.

4. FINISH: Stitch folded edges of binding tail together. Fold raw end under on back of stocking and stitch in place for hanger. Embellish ribbon with charms and tack to base of hanger.

1. Quilt, then cut out stocking

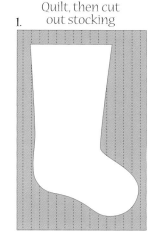

Stitch on pressed line / Flip & press / Trim & baste cuff, then applique

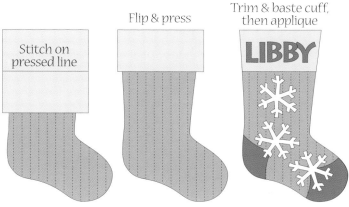

2.

3-4.

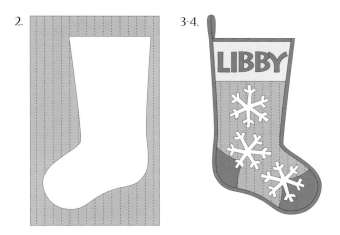

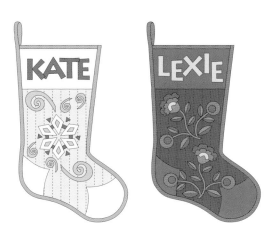

Stockings String Quilted Background

Photos on pages 11, 13   Finished length 20"

Directions make 1 diagonally oriented or 2 horizontally or vertically oriented stockings.

Materials   Choose fabric with 42" usable width.

Front	⅛ yd each of 12-15
Back	¾ yd
Cuff	⅜ yd
Lining	⅞ yd
Appliques	large scraps or ¼ yd pieces
Opt. tree panel	large scraps or ⅛ yd pieces of 3 fabrics (background, tree, trunk)
Binding	½ yd for 1 stocking (1 yd for 2 stockings)
Batting	1 square 25" & 1 piece 15 x 25" for 1 stocking (2 pieces 15 x 25" for 2 stockings)
Charms	1-2 yd narrow ribbon, dye-cut wood shapes, miniature ornaments, beads, buttons, bells

Cutting

Front	24-30 strips 1"-2½" wide by 25" long
Back	1 piece 15 x 25" for 1 stocking (2 pieces 15 x 25" for 2 stockings)
Cuff	1 square 10" for 1 stocking (2 squares 10" for 2)
Lining	1 square 25" & 1 piece 15 x 25" for 1 stocking (2 pieces 15 x 25" for 2 stockings)
Appliques	as desired - patterns on pages 49-55
Opt. tree panel	paper piecing pattern on page 52 cut 2 pieces 1¼ x 3⅜" & 2 pieces ¾ x 9¼" of tree background fabric
Binding	bias strips 2½" wide, pieced to 80" long for each stocking

Directions   Use ¼" seam allowance unless otherwise noted.

1. FRONT:

   Background: Place 25" square of lining wrong sides together with batting. String quilt from center toward both sides as shown. Cut out stocking front(s) as shown with toe(s) pointed the direction(s) shown.

   Cuff: Press cuff fabric in half wrong sides together. Open out and place right side down on stocking, matching raw edges at top. Stitch along pressed line. Flip lower part over to right side and press. Trim even with sides of stocking. Pin, then baste cuff in place ¼" from edge.

   Optional Tree Panel: Paper piece 3 trees. Stitch 3 blocks together. Stitch small background pieces to each end and long background pieces to top and bottom. Press long raw edge of each long background piece to back to cover seam allowance. Center sideways on stocking front, aligning top edge with placement line on pattern.

Topstitch panel to stocking along top and bottom edges. Trim even with side edges of stocking.

Applique: Applique stocking front using photos and diagrams as guides. Reduce letters on a copier for longer names, and/or overlap edges of letters if necessary to make name fit.

2. BACK: See Step 2 on page 43.

3. BIND: See Step 3 on page 43.

4. FINISH: See Step 4 on page 43.

1.   String quilt

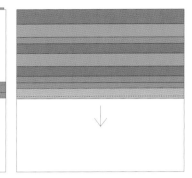

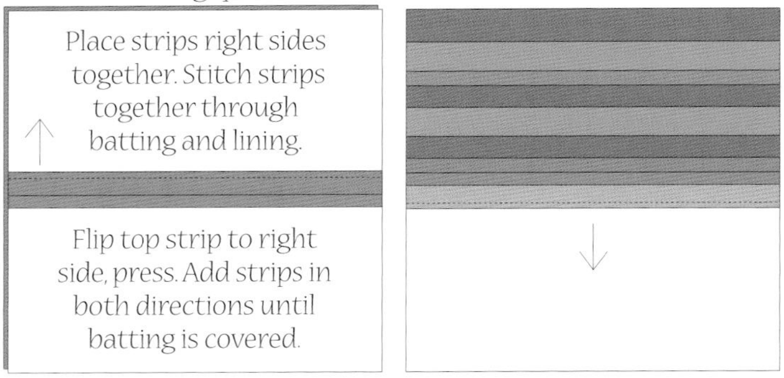

Place strips right sides together. Stitch strips together through batting and lining.

Flip top strip to right side, press. Add strips in both directions until batting is covered.

Cut out 1 diagonal stocking front

OR cut out 2 stocking fronts with horizontal or vertical strips

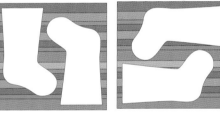

See diagrams on page 43 for cuff

Add tree panel & applique

2.

3-4.

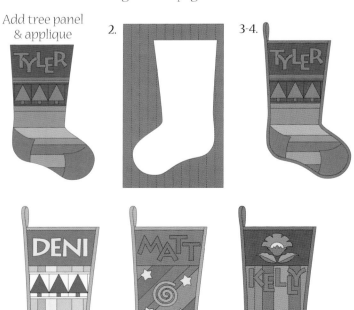

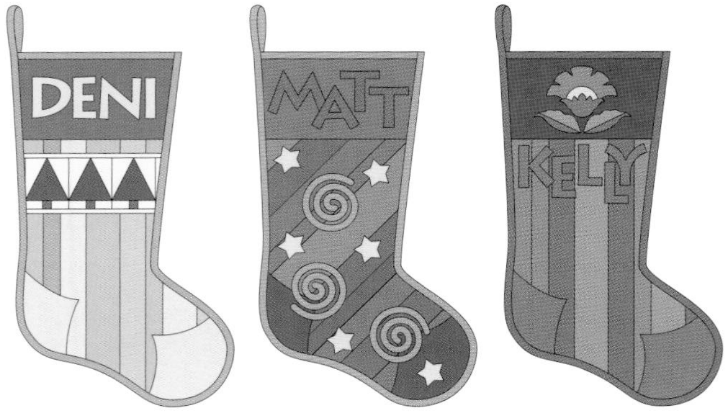

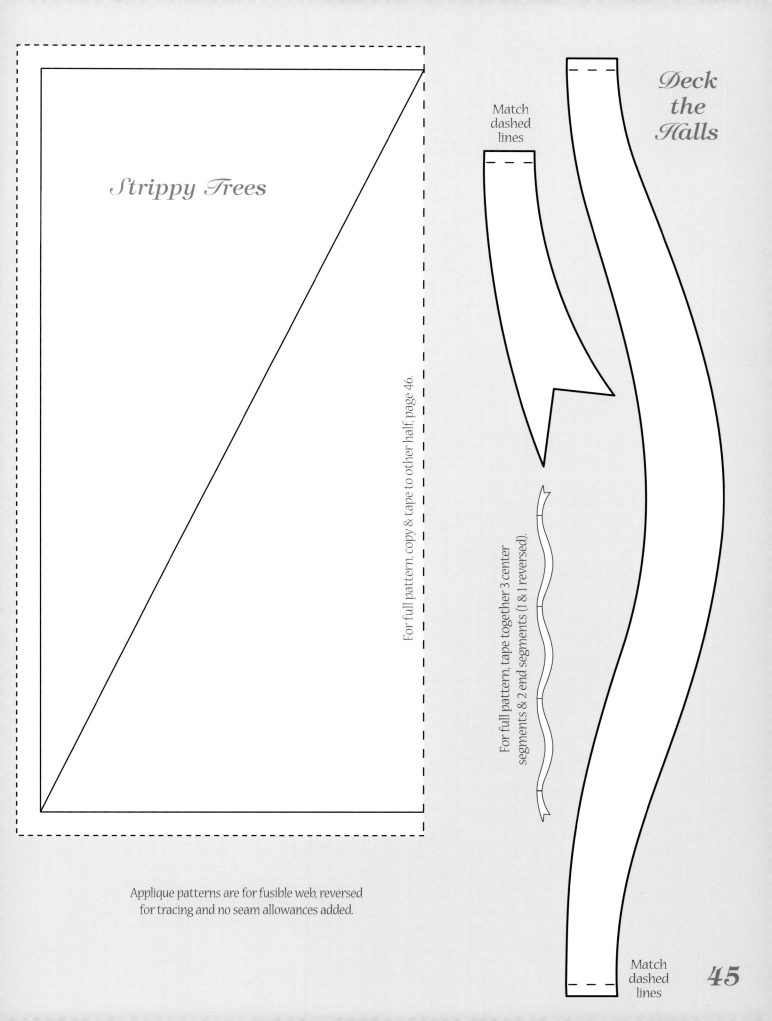

Strippy Trees

For full pattern, copy & tape to other half, page 46.

Applique patterns are for fusible web, reversed
for tracing and no seam allowances added.

Match
dashed
lines

*Deck
the
Halls*

For full pattern, tape together 3 center
segments & 2 end segments (1 & 1 reversed).

Match
dashed
lines

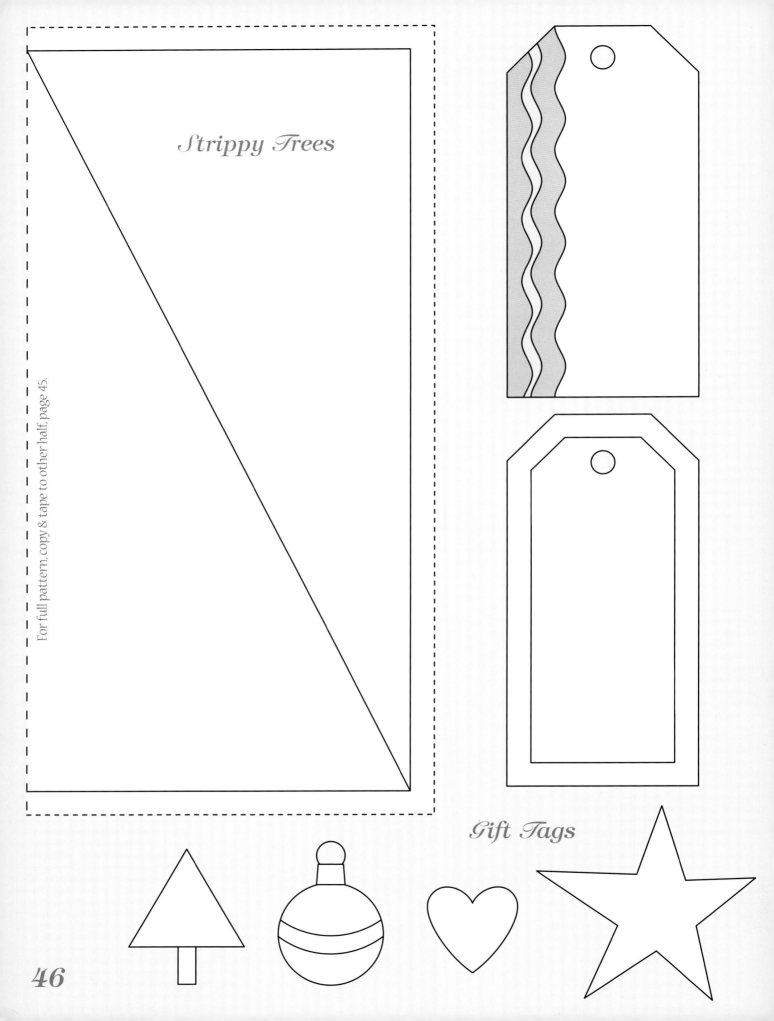

Strippy Trees

For full pattern, copy & tape to other half, page 45.

Gift Tags

46

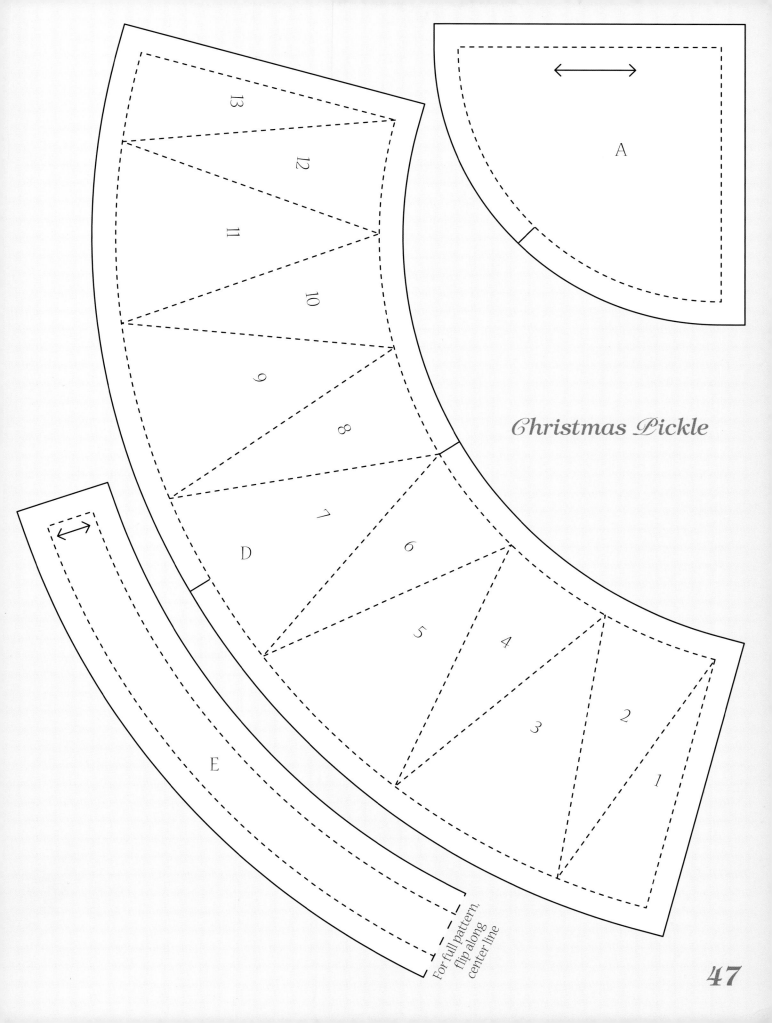

Christmas Pickle

A

13
12
11
10
9
8
7
6
5
4
3
2
1

D

E

For full pattern,
flip along
center line

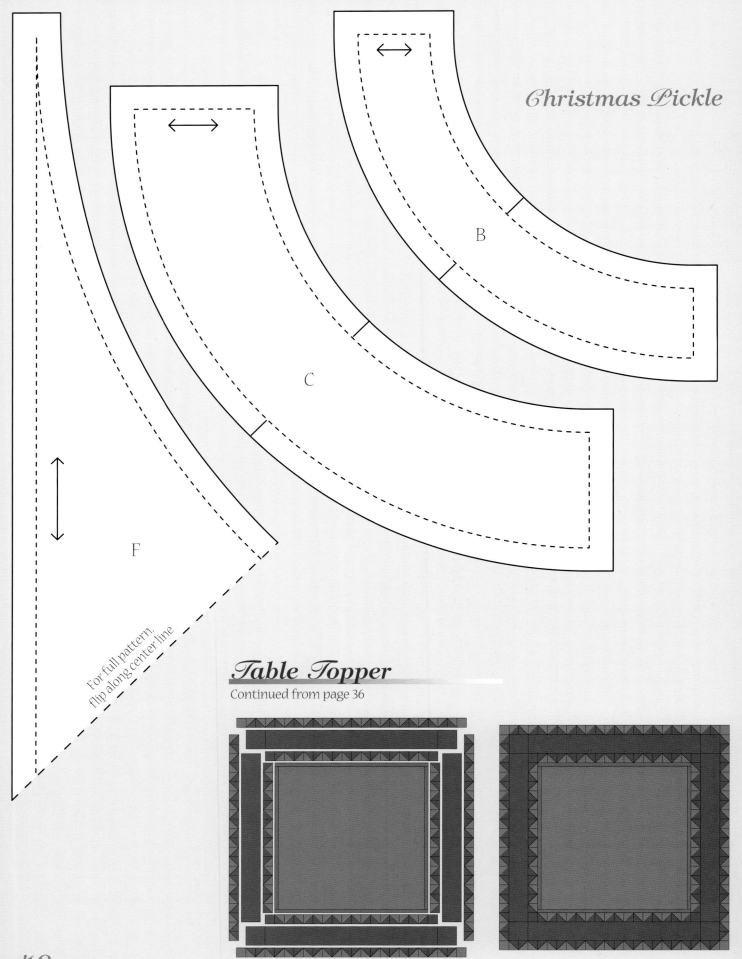

Christmas Pickle

B

C

F

For full pattern,
flip along center line

Table Topper

Continued from page 36

Stockings

Stockings

Top edge of tree panel

Make a 200% photocopy of the **whole page** for full-sized patterns.

NOTE: Copy to several sheets of paper, 11x17″ if possible, and tape the copies together.

Appliqué patterns are for fusible web, reversed for tracing and no seam allowances added.

49

Tree of Life
Welcome Friends

Stockings

Stockings

Applique patterns are for fusible web, reversed
for tracing and no seam allowances added.

Tree of Life

50

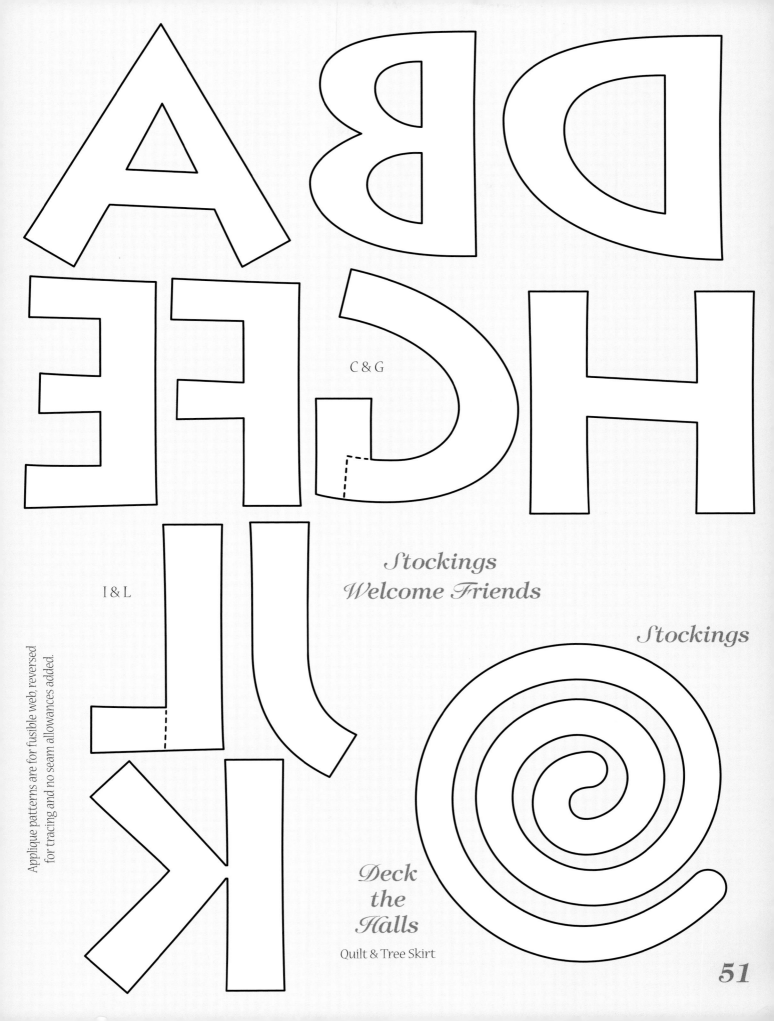

C & G

I & L

Applique patterns are for fusible web, reversed for tracing and no seam allowances added.

Stockings
Welcome Friends

Stockings

*Deck
the
Halls*

Quilt & Tree Skirt

51

M & W

O & Q

P & R

Stockings   *Welcome Friends*

Stockings

3   2

1

Stockings

3 1 2

Applique patterns are for fusible web, reversed for
tracing and no seam allowances added.

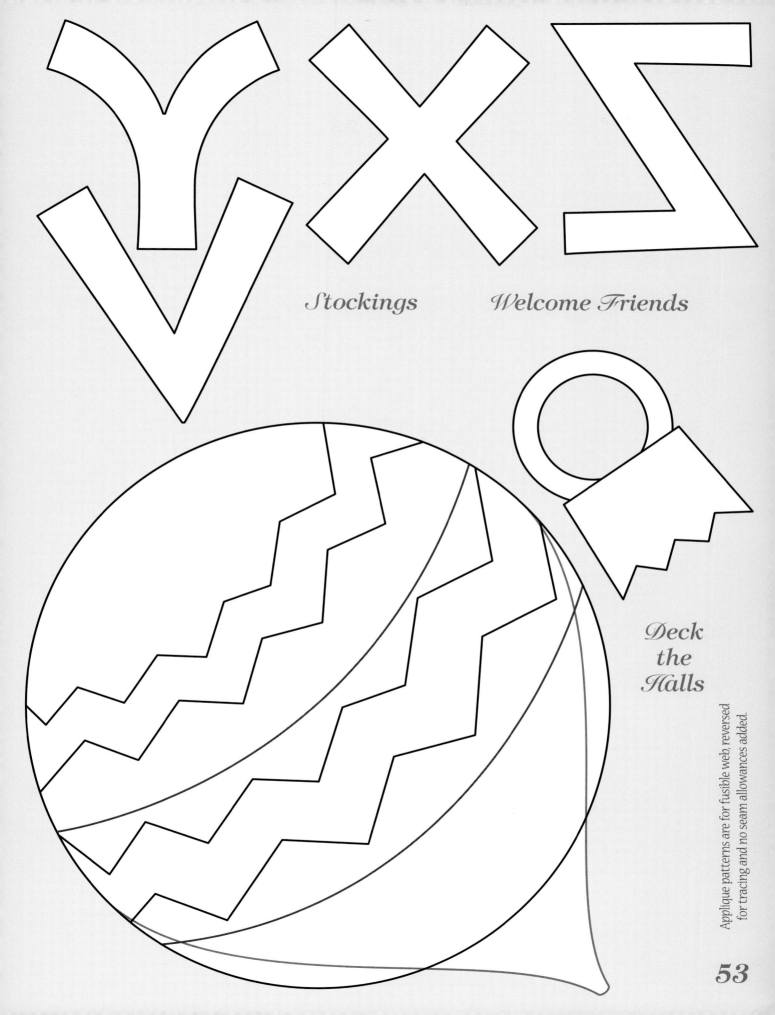

Stockings

Welcome Friends

Deck the Halls

Applique patterns are for fusible web, reversed for tracing and no seam allowances added.

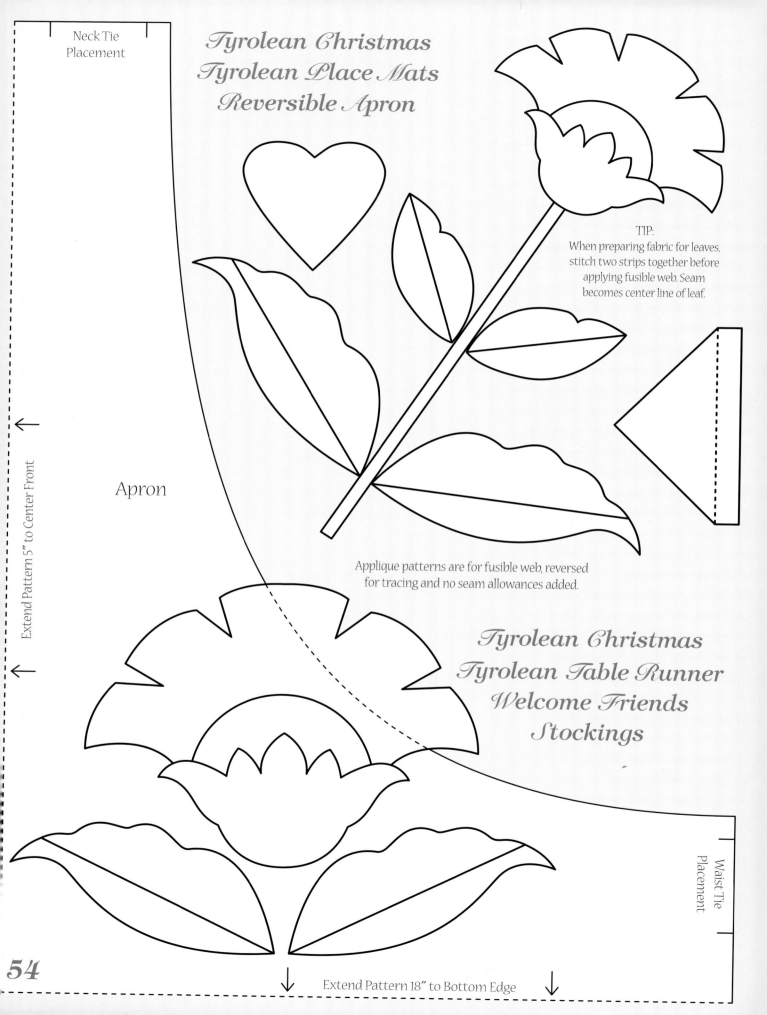

Tyrolean Christmas
Tyrolean Place Mats
Reversible Apron

TIP:
When preparing fabric for leaves, stitch two strips together before applying fusible web. Seam becomes center line of leaf.

Extend Pattern 5" to Center Front

Apron

Applique patterns are for fusible web, reversed for tracing and no seam allowances added.

Tyrolean Christmas
Tyrolean Table Runner
Welcome Friends
Stockings

Waist Tie Placement

Extend Pattern 18" to Bottom Edge

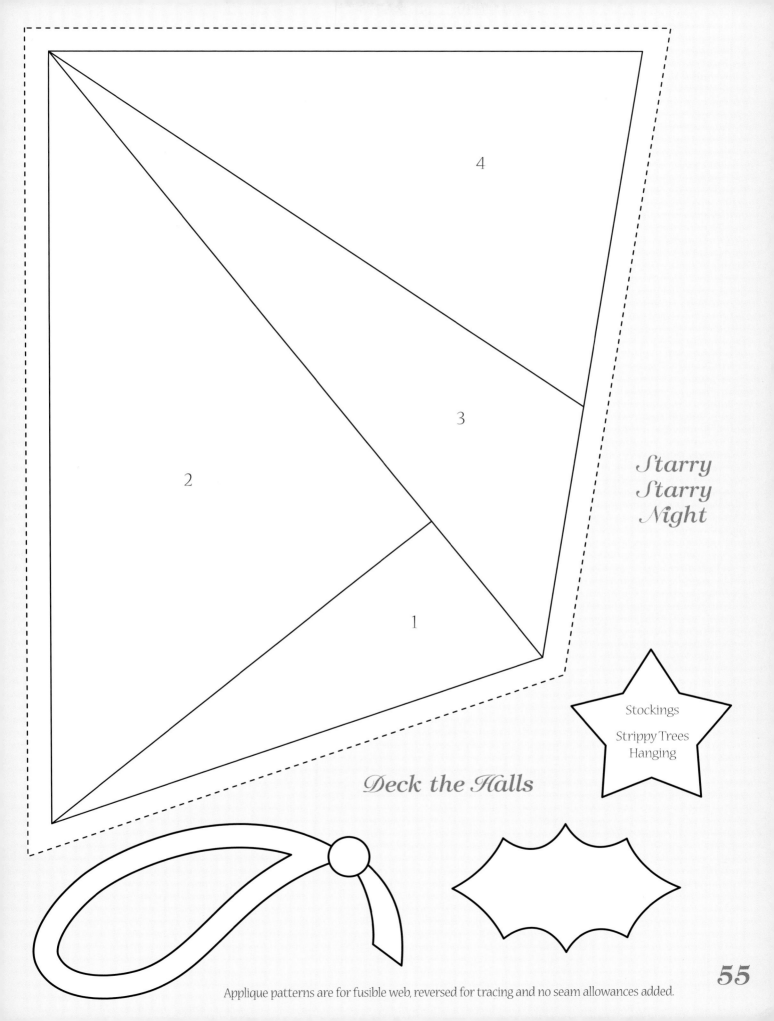

4

3

2

*Starry
Starry
Night*

1

Stockings

Strippy Trees
Hanging

Deck the Halls

Applique patterns are for fusible web, reversed for tracing and no seam allowances added.

Deck the Halls

Deck the Halls
Tree Skirt

Deck the Halls
Tree Skirt

Applique patterns are for fusible web, reversed for tracing and no seam allowances added.

1

Starry Starry Night

2

3

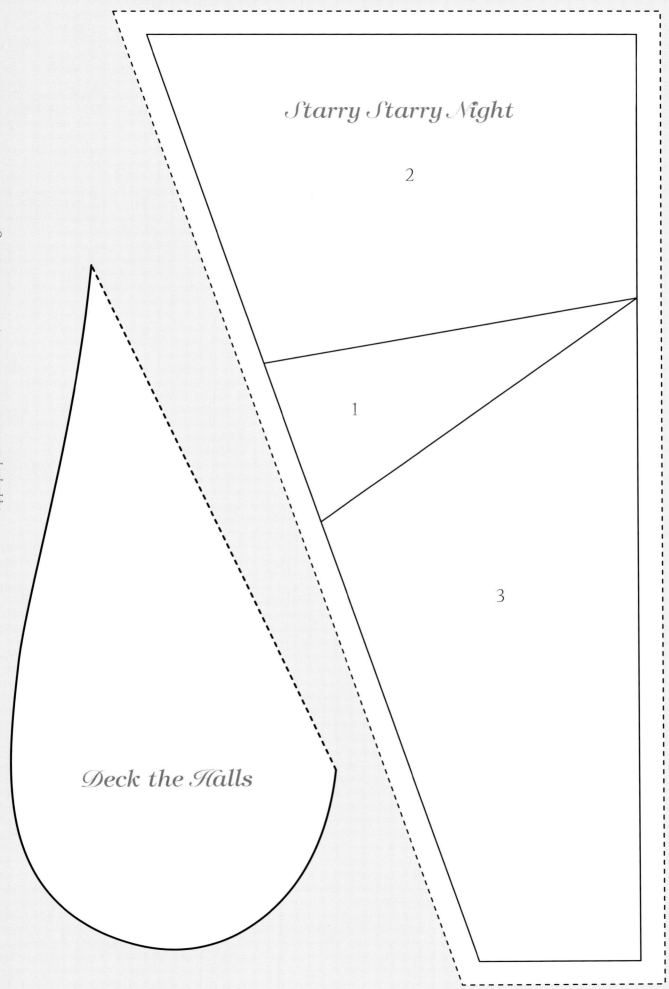

Starry Starry Night

2

1

3

Deck the Halls

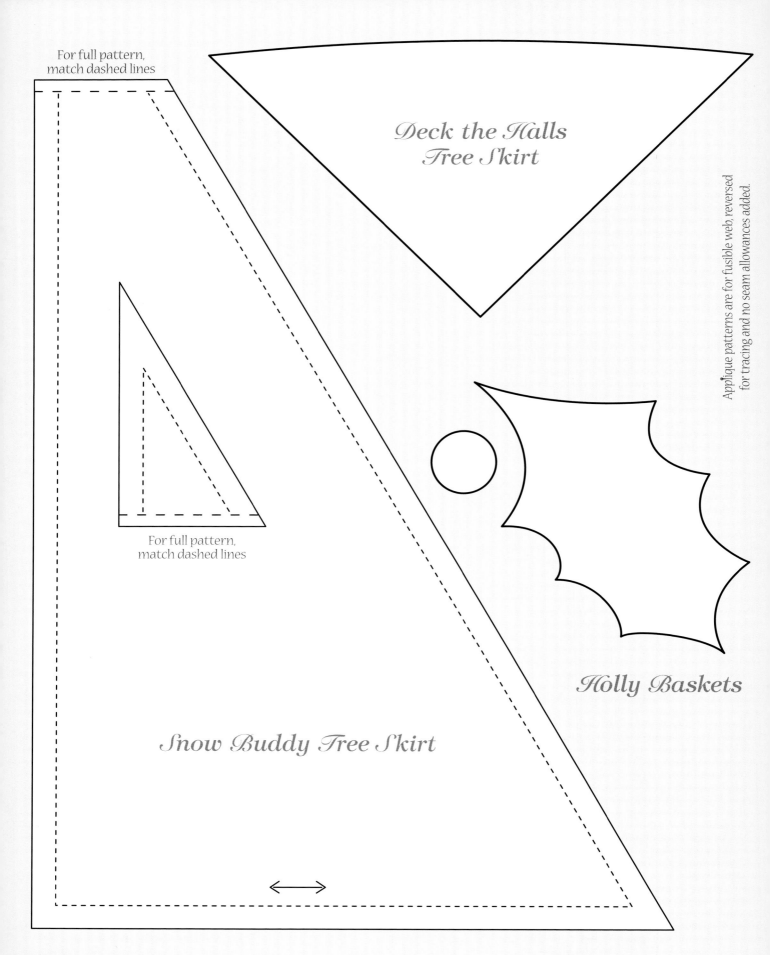

For full pattern,
match dashed lines

Deck the Halls
Tree Skirt

Applique patterns are for fusible web reversed
for tracing and no seam allowances added.

For full pattern,
match dashed lines

Holly Baskets

Snow Buddy Tree Skirt

Strippy Trees

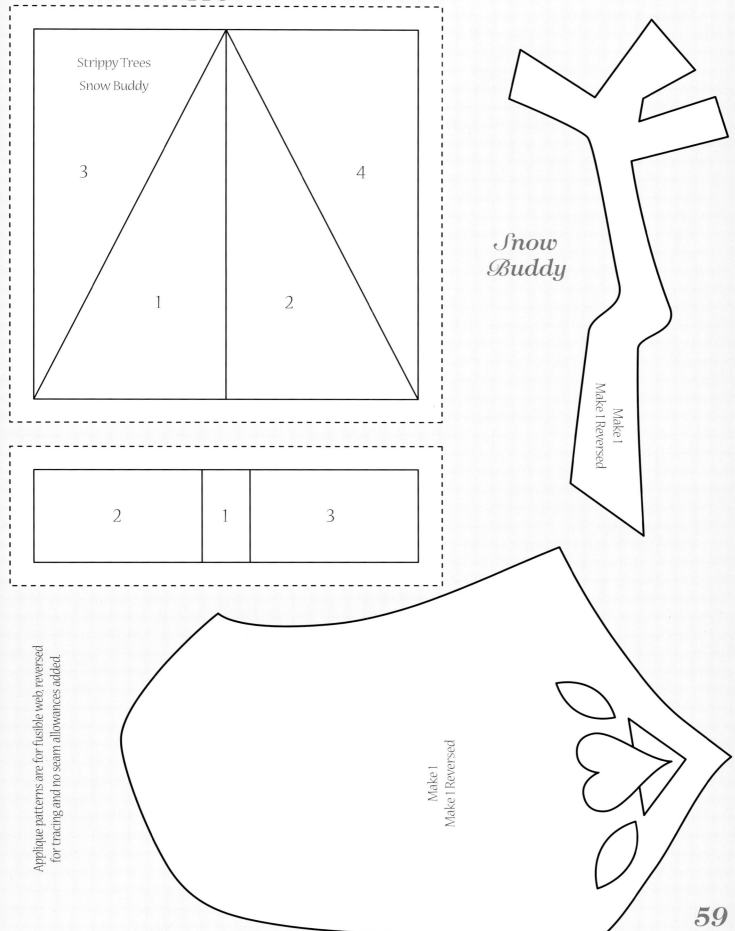

Strippy Trees
Snow Buddy

3

4

1

2

2

1

3

Snow Buddy

Make 1
Make 1 Reversed

Applique patterns are for fusible web, reversed for tracing and no seam allowances added.

Make 1
Make 1 Reversed

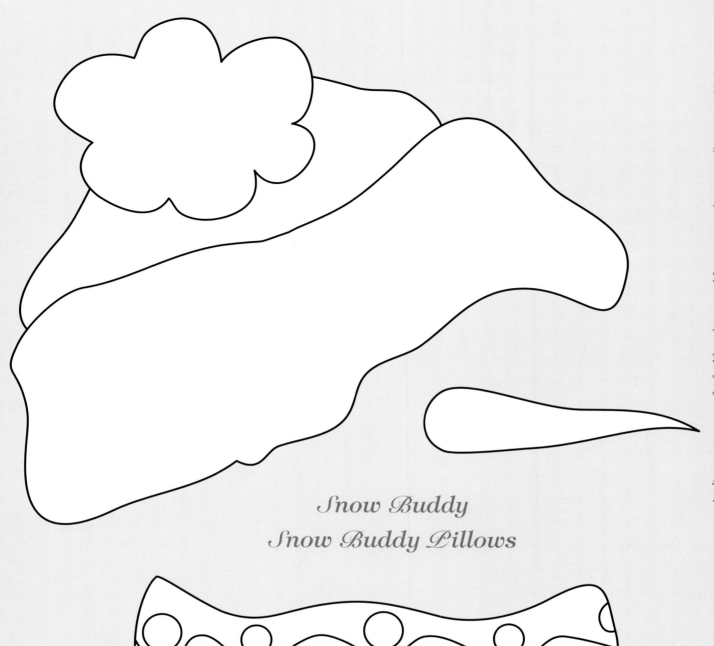

Snow Buddy
Snow Buddy Pillows

Applique patterns are for fusible web, reversed for tracing and no seam allowances added.

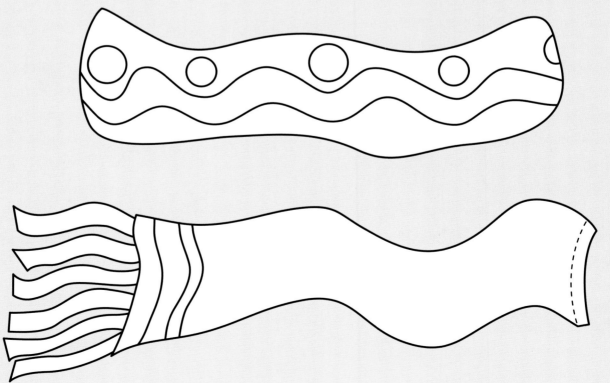